Alliance Academic Review

May 2001

Elio Cuccaro, Ph.D.
Editor

CHRISTIAN PUBLICATIONS, INC.
CAMP HILL, PENNSYLVANIA

Christian Publications, Inc.
3825 Hartzdale Drive
Camp Hill, PA 17011
www.cpi-horizon.com
www.christianpublications.com

Faithful, biblical publishing since 1883

Alliance Academic Review 2001
ISBN: 0-87509-933-5

Alliance
Academic Review

May 2001

To Alliance academics everywhere
for their contribution
to the advancement
of Christ's kingdom

Contents

Editorial: A Strategy for Promoting Our Pro-Life Stance ix

Preface xiii

Prophetic Politics or Moral Agitation?
Alan Keyes' Analogical Argument between Slavery and Abortion
Stephen Julian 1

Stewardship and the Kingdom of God
Ron Walborn and Frank Chan 25

Negative Jewish Reaction to Protestant Missions to the
Jews from the 1880s to Recent Days: Will It Ever End?
Daniel J. Evearitt 57

Premillennialism in the Medieval and Reformation Times
Harold P. Shelly 83

Beyond Fantasy: Tolkien, Lewis and Rowling
Richard Abanes 103

Providences and Providences
K. Neill Foster 119

About the Authors 127

Editorial

A Strategy for Promoting Our Pro-Life Stance

The General Council of 1981 adopted the following position statement on the moral issue of abortion:

> The moral issue of induced abortion ultimately involves a decision concerning those circumstances under which a human being may be permitted to take the life of another. We believe that life begins at conception and that this life is to be considered as human at that time.
>
> The C&MA believes that abortion on demand is morally wrong. We cannot allow the current social climate of moral relativism and sexual permissiveness to dictate our responses to moral and social dilemmas.
>
> The Word of God teaches that each individual is known by God from before the foundation of the world (Jeremiah 1:4-5, Psalm 139:13-17). Our Omnipotent, Omniscient, Omnipresent God has pronounced His blessing upon the life of a child according to Psalm 127:3-5.
>
> Since all life exists for God's purposes and all human lives are equally sacred, it is our belief that the life of the unborn child is blessed of God and must be preserved and nurtured. The C&MA is, therefore, opposed to induced abortion [only in the rarest instances, when it is impossible to save the life of both the mother and the child, should the question of an induced abortion be considered]. (*Manual*, 1999, p. G4-1)

Since America is pretty well split down the middle on this subject, with avid pro-choice forces entrenched on one side and determined pro-life forces dug in on the other, the likelihood of continuing stalemate and polarization is real. How do we move beyond this impasse to best foster and promote our pro-life view? It would seem that some strategy is in order.

A thought-through strategy for such promotion, however, requires a prior position on the issue of church and state or Christ and culture—a matter unaddressed by any Alliance position statement. For example, if we aligned ourselves with the Anabaptist idea of a thorough separation of church and state, we would limit our strategy to inculcating in our own Christian people the sanctity of life. The goal would be to eliminate abortions among Christians. The state would be left to do whatever it pleased. It would be abandoned to its own sinful outlook and legally sanctioned abortion practices. The only transformation going on would coincide with the growth of the pro-life consensus in the church. In this view, the church and the state represent two distinct and separate kingdoms. Christians ought only to concern themselves with their faithfulness to membership in the kingdom of God. The only thing that we owe secular society is a consistent testimony in word and life of what we believe so that the way to life (and secondarily, to a right understanding of abortion) is open to all.

Another more idealized church-and-state construct is the coincidence model presented in Thomas More's *Utopia* and Martin Bucer's *The Kingdom of Christ*. Here there is a convergence of secular government and ecclesiastical authority so that all laws are an outworking of the commands of God. This is simultaneously and coincidentally the Christian state and the kingdom of Christ. In this view, an appropriate strategy would be to have the pro-life stance enacted into law. The standardization of the will of God into appropriate legal prescriptions would serve the greatest possible interest of the Christian citizenry. Moreover, God would be completely honored in this thoroughly Christian kingdom. Clearly, if the first model errs in taking separation to abandonment, the second model would be anathema to a pluralistic society.

A third church-and-state model is provided by the reformer Martin Luther, who advocated a scheme of two overlapping kingdoms. The state operated by force of arms and had within its proper sphere of influence areas such as defense, justice, common order and the common welfare. The church operated by moral suasion and labored within its sphere of influence in spiritual and moral transformation, works of mercy and the common welfare. Where there was an overlapping, common welfare interest (such as education or relief of poverty or marriage), influence and persuasion worked in both directions. But in the sphere unique to each, the church did not tell the state how to use the sword, and the state did not interfere in the preaching of the gospel. Every citizen was a member of two kingdoms and rendered unto Caesar what was Caesar's and unto God what was God's. In this view, abortion would be an overlapping, common welfare interest. A strategy of moral suasion to persuade the state and the populace of the compelling tragedy of abortion and the moral superiority of the pro-life stance would be in order.

I believe that this third model offers American Christians the only workable construct, given our dual realities of a strong Christian tradition and a secular, pluralistic state. All believing Christians, then, are citizens of the United States and members of the kingdom of God. While spiritual good may belong to them as Christians, their temporal good is generally tied to the temporal good of everyone in this great land. Therefore, a strategy to seek the common welfare consistent with our position statement on abortion is the good and responsible contribution of Christians to all of society.

Here, then, are my components for a pro-life strategy for our church in the United States:

1. Build a strong Christian consensus on this issue so that we come close to speaking with one voice. The intense interest in stopping abortions should be directed first toward the household of faith. If we cannot persuade other Christians not to have abortions, how can we persuade unbelievers? Alternatives to abortion must be broadened here so that the people who make the argument for abortion alternatives are ready to be a part of the solution.

2. Speak to power with moral authority. Every Christian is represented by elected representatives in state and federal government. As good citizens of the state, it is our responsibility (for the common welfare) to make sure that our views are heard and are taken into account.

3. Make common cause with those who agree with us and are willing to work with us on this issue. For example, individual Catholic pro-life advocates, such as Alan Keyes (see Stephen Julian's article on him in

this issue) or the Roman Catholic hierarchy may be happy to stand with us. It is no compromise of our kingdom faith if, as citizens of the state, we work with other concerned citizens to accomplish common welfare goals.

4. Accept incremental progress as a way of moving toward the final goal. It may be that parental notification, waiting periods, required counseling on abortion alternatives and similar limiting measures are all that can be passed for now. Roman Catholic hospitals recently faced down the federal government by refusing to allow their facilities to perform abortions. It appears that there is already sufficient congressional support to soon enact a restriction on partial birth abortions. Small progress is still progress. As the Spirit of God said, we should not despise the days of small beginnings (Zechariah 4:10).

Preface

The *Alliance Academic Review*, first issued at Council '95, is an anthology dedicated to and composed mostly by Alliance academics around the world. Comparable writing by other Alliance members is welcome. The common virtue of all writing shall be that it is consistent with and promotive of the biblical message, the ministry and the mission of The Christian and Missionary Alliance. The *Review* intends to publish, disseminate and keep in print the best work of our academic research.

To be inclusive of all theologically related disciplines, a sincere effort shall be made to accept an equal number of papers from the following five academic divisions:

1. Alliance Heritage/Church History

2. Biblical/Theological Studies

3. Church Ministries

4. Missions

5. Religion and Society/Integration of Faith and Learning

Articles submitted may have been recently published elsewhere, recently delivered orally or specifically written for the *Review*. Each is expected to be well-researched, presented and documented. The esoteric and technical should be avoided or, at least, relegated to the endnotes. *The Chicago Manual of Style*, Fourteenth Edition, is the writing style standard. It shall be the responsibility of the writer to secure copyright permission for prepublished material submitted.

Articles and correspondence should be directed to the managing editor:

David E. Fessenden
Christian Publications, Inc.
3825 Hartzdale Drive
Camp Hill, PA 17011
E-mail: editors@cpi-horizon.com

The authors of accepted articles will be rewarded with a modest stipend. Articles not chosen will be retained on file for possible future use, unless their return is requested.

As long as the *Review* elicits a favorable response, it will be continued as an annual series.

In This Issue

The first article by Stephen Julian is a piece on a particularly interesting recent chapter in religion and society: the moral crusade of 1996 and 2000 presidential candidate Alan Keyes. More specifically, Julian analyzes Keyes' most powerful pro-life argument; namely, that the slavery of the last century is comparable to the abortion holocaust since the Roe v. Wade Supreme Court decision.

The second paper is a biblical study on stewardship written for the Alliance by Ronald Walborn and Frank Chan. It sets out to reclaim and reassert the biblical teaching that should guide our earning, spending, saving and giving as committed disciples and stewards in the kingdom of God.

The third article by Daniel Evearitt reviews the reception that Jews have given to Protestant missions to the Jews since the time of the founding of the C&MA. The reception has never been good, but the most bitter reaction has been reserved for Messianic Jews' (such as Jews for Jesus) efforts to convert other Jews.

The last three articles are excerpted from current or upcoming books. The first is from a future volume on the theme of millennialism. Harold Shelly treats the view of millennialism advocated during the Middle Ages and the Reformation. There was some premillennialism, however rare, even in those days, and Shelly does a good job of showing its presence. In a chapter from *Harry Potter and the Bible*, Richard Abanes examines the similarities—and differences—between the best-selling Harry Potter series and various classic fantasy novels for children.

And finally, K. Neill Foster, in a selection from his latest book, *Sorting Out the Supernatural*, discusses the distinction between providences from God and "providences" from other sources.

Prophetic Politics or Moral Agitation? Alan Keyes' Analogical Argument between Slavery and Abortion

Stephen Julian

In 1996, Alan Keyes' address to an audience in New Hampshire was quickly broadcast on the syndicated radio show "Focus on the Family" and then, after the program was flooded with requests, was repeated again the next day. Keyes' speech was the first time the show had played the same material two days in a row. Keyes is an anomaly. He is a black Catholic Republican with a Harvard Ph.D. He represents to many the potential for a conservative shift by both blacks and Catholics to the Republican Party. In the case of Catholics, the shift began with the Reagan Democrats who supported conservative social issues.[1] For blacks, the emergence of a conservative voting bloc has yet to materialize. Keyes brings to life the commitment of socially conservative Catholics and evangelical Protestants to work together on issues such as abortion.[2]

This paper examines the rhetorical strategies of Keyes in his 1996 presidential campaign. I claim that Keyes uses his arguments and style to draw together his natural base of support: evangelical Protestants and socially conservative Catholics. He does this by making public morality the focus of his campaign and by making abortion the most visible aspect of that morality. Keyes develops an analogy between slavery and abortion as the basis for his argument against abortion. I argue that his analogy is politically problematic, suggesting that Keyes should adopt the role of a moral agitator rather than a politician.

1

Keyes' Argument against Abortion

Keyes' argument against abortion is straightforward:

1. The Declaration of Independence recognizes the fundamental human rights of all persons when it says: "We hold these truths to be self-evident, that all men are created equal, that they are endowed by their Creator with certain unalienable rights, that among these are life, liberty and the pursuit of happiness."
2. Our equality as humans means that no person's rights may justly supersede those of another unless there is a clear hierarchy to the two rights and the higher right is upheld.
3. In its recognition of our fundamental human rights, the Declaration acknowledges God, our Creator, as the source of our rights and as the only person who can properly define who will count as human; that is, who will be the rightful possessor of these rights.
4. Therefore, abortion is a struggle between the rights of the mother and the rights of her offspring. The most fundamental right, the right to life, must supersede all others. Thus, only in the case of the endangerment of the mother's life can her rights legitimately offset the offspring's right to life.

Saying that the argument is straightforward, is not to say that it is unproblematic. The second premise concerning the hierarchy of rights is probably the least controversial of these four claims, and one can see how quickly an argument over this hierarchy would emerge. In response to the first premise, some certainly would see the Declaration as creating a view of human rights rather than merely reporting a preexisting condition. Many would object to the claim in the final premise that there is a God. Even theists might reject the notion that we must rely upon God for our rights and the definition of those to whom they apply. The conclusion is problematic because it assumes that which it must prove—namely that that which is aborted is properly deemed a human being. Thus, we find ourselves quickly sinking into the quagmire of this ongoing debate.

Despite these potential objections, what makes Keyes' argument compelling to so many listeners? The most obvious answer is that they are already convinced of his conclusion and therefore simply see the argument as reinforcing their perspective. More subtly, however, Keyes attempts to bolster the rhetorical appeal of this argument by insisting that abortion is the modern-day analogy to slavery. Slavery was an instance where a clash of human rights resulted in the immoral subjugation of one party's fundamental rights to the lesser rights of another. Abortion, he contends, involves a similar clash of rights.

Keyes' Personal Ethos as a Black American

This analogy serves to strategically position Keyes on the issue of abortion. First, it allows him, a black American, to build on his personal ethos as a descendant of slaves, thereby making his argument more difficult to challenge. When addressing Black Americans for Life, Keyes attacks Colin Powell for having said "that he grew up with a strong sense of self-worth because he did not look back to the heritage of slavery, [since] he was of Jamaican ancestry. Now I've got to tell you that being from that group of Americans who does look back to the heritage of slavery. . . . I hope nobody will misunderstand it if I took offense at that statement!"

Keyes attacks Powell as pro-choice and argues that Powell has adopted this position, at least in part, because he does not understand the relevance of the slavery analogy:

> I do not understand how anyone who looks back on that heritage, and knows that that injustice came from the principle that lies at the heart of this abortion rights movement, how can anyone then stand on the same side as those who are resurrecting the principle of oppression and slavery that destroyed my Black Ancestors!!! [sic] It does not make any sense.[3]

Keyes identifies with the victims of abortion and argues that an appreciation for the suffering of black Americans will allow others to participate in this identification. He uses a similar approach when speaking to a Jewish audience. He tells them that the same injustice that allowed Nazis to define Jews as less than human is behind the atrocity of abortion. Of course, one of the typical arguments used by women to silence their male opposition is that men do not get pregnant and so this is a decision women must make in private. This underscores the perception that this is a religious or moral issue in the sense of being subjective and personal.

When Wolf Blitzer interviewed Keyes, he asked Keyes how he, as a man, could tell a woman she did not have the right to an abortion. Keyes replied:

> Oh, I don't have that right. And I'm not telling anybody anything. I simply read the words of the American Declaration of Independence, which say quite clearly, "All men are created equal, they are endowed by their Creator"—not by decision of the mother, not by a woman's choice—but by their Creator, they get their humanity. And we cannot be saying that we will set the woman's will higher than God's will because our Declaration says that that's not so. So I am not making any decision. The Declaration of Independence states the principle and as a people, we must abide by it. It's that simple.[4]

So Keyes resists the role of oppressor and takes on that of the victim in his opposition to abortion. Later in the paper I will discuss the tension between his emphasis upon God's role in the argument and his attempt to downplay any particular religious position. That is, he uses our common civic religion to counter claims that taking God seriously necessarily involves that which is personal and subjective.

Thus, while the argument against abortion, or slavery for that matter, should be color-blind (since it is about human rights generally and not about the rights of any group in particular), Keyes uses his heritage to argue that he better understands the horrors of allowing humans to decide who will count as fellow human beings. In addition, Keyes' style cultivates the image of him as a black minister, conveying an impression of moral power. Those who respond to him, supporters and detractors alike, often refer to his conviction and eloquence. He recognizes this image of himself in the following:

> Now of course there are going to be those people who say: "Well, Preacher, that sounds pretty good, but I thought you were a politician. I didn't know this was a pulpit." Now I have to tell you, there are those folks who remember every now and again that Teddy Roosevelt was right and that the Presidency is a bully pul-

pit. And it would be a good idea every now and again
to put somebody in it who knows how to use it.[5]

Here the secularized bully pulpit of Roosevelt is linked to the image of the prophetic (i.e., in the sense of forth-telling) voice calling out, "Thus saith the Lord."

This image cuts both ways. If Keyes is not careful, his rhetoric could feed into the impression that this really is a fundamentally religious issue; that is, an issue that is personal, subjective and potentially arbitrary. As George McKenna points out in "On Abortion: A Lincolnian Position," Stephen Douglas used the tactic of equating religion with personal preference in his response to the issue of slavery:

> I am now speaking of rights under the Constitution, and not of moral or religious rights. I do not discuss the morals of the people of Missouri, but let them settle that matter for themselves. I hold that the people of the slaveholding States are civilized men as well as ourselves, that they bear consciences as well as we, and that they are accountable to God and their posterity and not to us. It is for them to decide therefore the moral and religious right of the slavery question for themselves within their own limits.[6]

McKenna writes, "In this view, religion is largely a matter of taste, and to impose one's taste upon another is not only repressive but also irrational."[7] Therefore, conveying an impression of conviction may cause the listener to listen more closely, but may also lead him to consider the eloquence as an expression of personal conviction rather than public morality. For Keyes to succeed, he must be seen as articulating that which is true for everyone rather than merely the truth as he sees it.

Borrowing the Ethos of Lincoln

Therefore, Keyes attempts to use the analogy to slavery not only to utilize his ethos as a black American, but also to connect him with a tradition of like-minded Americans. Specifically, it allows him to draw upon one of the most potent images in American history: Abraham Lincoln. The image of Lincoln has been painted from numerous angles, but Keyes dusts off the most familiar portrait of Lincoln as the emancipator, as someone thoroughly convinced of the evil of slavery. Keyes argues that even Lincoln's political pragmatism could not keep him in the end from doing that which was just.

When challenged by a listener to consider the prudential example of Lincoln as striking a compromise on the issue of slavery, calling for the restriction of its growth rather than for its abolition, Keyes responds as follows:

> You've missed the point of Lincoln's statesmanship. . . . We are being tempted to go down a road that says, "OK, let's accept Roe vs. Wade, its premises and so forth, and see whether we can't operate within that to reduce this evil, and so forth." That's not a Lincolnian position. The Lincoln position is to make it very clear what the right and wrong of it is. And when you have made that very clear and re-established the basic principle on which the country must approach the issue, then you can talk about those areas where some of the evil may be tolerated in order that the rest of the good that we certainly know this society represents can be preserved. But you don't allow the wellspring of your freedom to be poisoned, because if you do the Republic dies.[8]

Here Keyes articulates the strategy used by Garrisonian immediatists to combat slavery: call for the absolute on principle and then use that call to move the opposition closer to your position.

Aileen Kraditor has written an astute analysis of Garrisonian immediatism, entitled *Means and Ends in American Abolitionism*. Central to her book are two insights. First, Garrison and other radical abolitionists were committed to achieving two goals: ending slavery and eradicating racism. Garrison recognized that these two issues were intertwined in such a way that eradicating racism would necessarily lead to the end of slavery, but ending slavery would not necessarily result in the eradication of racism. Consequently, the primary goal for radical abolitionists was to appeal to white Americans on a moral plane rather than concentrating efforts in the political arena where it was quite possible that the institution could be undermined without altering racist perceptions of blacks.

In a similar fashion, Keyes is attempting to undermine the philosophical and moral basis for the right to abort rather than merely calling for its legal prohibition. Without a change in moral sensibility, no law will have the desired effect. Back alley abortions pose a threat not just to pro-choice advocates, but to pro-lifers who genuinely desire to see the motivation for abortion made impossible to defend.

A second insight that Kraditor provides is emphasized in the title she chose: *Means and Ends in American Abolitionism.* Kraditor points out that Garrison's principled insistence on immediatism had often been criticized as impractical and detrimental to the antislavery cause. Kraditor's interpretation gives Garrison greater, but not uncritical, credit as a rhetorical tactician. She views Garrison's immediatism as a rhetorical strategy: "In addition to being the 'end' of the movement, [the slogan of immediate and unconditional emancipation] was also a means; in fact, throughout the life of the movement, it was used primarily as a means, a tool for reaching the conscience of the hearer."[9] As to the practicality of these means, she writes:

> If politics is the art of the possible, agitation is the art of the desirable. The practice of each must be judged by criteria appropriate to its goal. Agitation by the reformer or radical helps define one possible policy as more desirable than another, and if skillful and uncompromising, the agitation may help make the desirable possible. To criticize the agitator for not trimming his demands to the immediately realizable—that is, for not acting as a politician—is to miss the point.[10]

In similar fashion, Keyes' call for a constitutional amendment banning abortion, except in cases where the mother's life is endangered, can be seen as an attempt to challenge from a position of absolute principle. One difference, however, is that Keyes is a politician, and he cannot help but think like a politician at times. When faced with the question of whether he would accept a provision allowing abortions in cases of rape and incest, he says,

> Now see, I can see no grounds for making exceptions in the case of rape and incest. Why would you be taking the crime of the father out on the child, giving

7

them the death penalty because their father committed rape. If we have to regard, as I think we must, under God's law, as our declaration said, we have to regard that human life as possessing the unalienable right to life. The circumstances of that situation don't take that right away.[11]

In a letter to one of his supporters, however, Keyes writes,

> I make an exception only for the physical life of the mother. Given the unalienable right to life (i.e., self-preservation) I see no way in principle to avoid making this exception. I would accept the rape and incest exceptions only as a matter of political necessity if that is the best legislation we could achieve at the time (precisely the circumstances you allude to in your message). I see no grounds in principle for making these exceptions, but I do regard people who, for emotional reasons, make them (such as George Bush) fellow pro-lifers. As a matter of political prudence it would be suicidal for the pro-life movement to reject these people. Though I disagree with them in principle, I will not pursue that disagreement in such a way as to lead the pro-life movement toward political suicide.[12]

It is this sort of statement which distances a Keyes from a Garrison; a politician from a professional agitator. Garrison repeatedly threatened the viability of the abolitionist movement in an attempt to retain the absolute focus of the immediatists. I will return to this issue when I discuss the weaknesses of Keyes' approach.

Recalling the Birth of the Republican Party

Just as Keyes builds upon the ethos of Lincoln, so he draws upon the history of the Republican party to support his case:

> And I can tell you right now that those who are recommending that we pull the pro-life plank out of the Republican Party platform are recommending that (as

some people decided in the Whig Party in the years before the Civil War that they would be silent on the great issue of principle that faced this nation) we shall be silent. And you see what happened to the Whigs. The Republican Party grew up as a party aimed at dealing with that moral irresponsibility, standing on the principle that Lincoln articulated—that you cannot have the right to do what is wrong.[13]

Keyes calls the party to return to its roots. As he states it,

This Party was born on a clear commitment to principle. This party was born of those who had the courage to stand before the American people and in the, in the face of the threat of a greater division than we'll ever face, insist that we had to respect the principles that make us great, the principles that make us strong, the principles that make us free. And I'll tell you, we're going to have to do it again.[14]

The reference to the Civil War as "a greater division than we'll ever face" brings to mind a recurring criticism of Keyes. He is repeatedly charged with dividing the Republican Party by arguing so strongly for his position. Keyes responds, as do most pro-life Republicans, that it is they who have brought renewed vigor to the party and if anyone is tearing it apart it is those who deny the moral basis of the party. He compares the pro-choice Republicans to the Whigs who will destroy the party in an abortive attempt to avoid facing the central moral issue of the day.

Garrison was often attacked as dividing the abolitionist movement, and there is little doubt that he did just that, but as an agitator who argued from principle, he felt it was his duty to hold fast regardless of the fallout from his position. Keyes, by contrast, tries to draw upon the history of the Republican Party and the analogy to its antislavery stance to claim that he is standing fast with its founders and that it is the pro-choice faction that is precipitating a split. Rather than settling for a defensive posture, he goes on the offensive and paints his opposition as the inheritors of a political tradition that suffocates rather than revives the party's life.

Keyes paints the pro-lifers as the victors, not merely in some eventual sense, but as having already won the decisive battle in this war. For evidence he points to key proponents of the pro-choice position who have begun to acknowledge publicly the undesirability of abortion, even the moral wrongness of it.

> I can tell that we have won this battle because the man right now who is the champion of the pro-abortion cause (sitting there in the White House) has told us that abortion should be, "safe, legal, and rare." Well if it's good, why does he want it rare? If it's just, why does he want it rare? If it's not evil, why does he want it rare? Because in his conscience he knows that it's wrong. Now of course if he's listening to his wife (she gave an interview in *Newsweek* or wherever it was) and she said, "It's wrong, abortion is wrong." And he appointed Henry Foster who had done all these abortions and what does he stand up and say? "I abhor abortion." You don't abhor something that's right, do you? Generally speaking I don't, do you? No. You see, the battle for America's conscience is over.[15]

Keyes knows that political victory without moral conversion is meaningless and he argues that the moral recognition of abortion as wrong has begun taking place so that what remains is to defeat it politically.

To make the analogy to slavery explicit, he goes on to say,

> And just as by the time you get to the 1850s most decent-minded Americans had decided that slavery was wrong, so most decent-minded Americans have decided and know in their heart that abortion is morally wrong. We have won that battle. . . . People know it's wrong. But the problem we have now, my friends, is that folks want to deny that it is a public wrong, you see. They do. And the other day during this partial-birth abortion debate they had a lady on who had had this "medical procedure." And she was saying that she thought that this was a "private decision" and so forth and so on. And even my daugh-

ter Maya (10 years old, and of good heart) could hear that and understand that, as she put it, that would be like saying that we could take her upstairs in the bedroom and murder her and that would just be a private moment. You see, nobody believes this. But that's what we're saying. We're saying that it's a private judgment.[16]

Keyes focuses on this privacy argument and claims that enslaving someone else is not a private matter; murdering his daughter in her bedroom is not a private matter; therefore, taking the life of an unborn child is not a private matter. All of these are matters of public morality even if the acts take place in privacy. It is critical that just as slavery was acknowledged as personal and public evil, so abortion must be seen as wrong for all, regardless of their personal beliefs. It is the analogy of the slave to the fetus that Keyes must make plausible, and this brings us back to the document upon which his argument rests.

Emphasizing the Declaration of Independence

The decision to emphasize the Declaration over the Constitution is a strategy that has been employed by numerous Americans in a variety of conflicts, most notably in the abolitionists' opposition to slavery. Garrison burned a copy of the Constitution which he saw as a morally corrupt document, complicitous in the evil of slavery. He venerated the Declaration for much the same reasons as Keyes, as the document articulating the fundamental rights of humans. Focusing on the Declaration also shifts the argument away from the vicissitudes of a governing document to a document that remains unchanged, one that merely articulates pre-existing truth—a truth that while central to the founding of this nation is one that transcends this nation's boundaries. But Keyes' reading of this document will be compelling only if one accepts his emphasis upon God. He sees human attempts to define "humanity" as leading to disastrous consequences and believes that these efforts arrogate the authority which belongs to God alone. Our role is simply to acknowledge that which God has decided as our creator. Before turning to the potential problems of Keyes' theism, I will point to one final benefit of the slavery analogy.

11

Focusing on Principle Rather than Practice

Keyes maintains that slavery was wrong regardless of how the slaves were treated physically. The horror of slavery is that one person believes he has the right to own another human being. Similarly, abortion is wrong regardless of how it is accomplished. The horror of abortion is that one person believes she has the right to terminate the life of another human being. This is an important aspect of Keyes' position because it anticipates a shift in the abortion debate as RU-486 and other nonsurgical abortion techniques draw attention away from centralized, physically locatable abortion clinics and spread abortion amorphously into innumerable doctors' offices and private homes.

When speaking to Black Americans for Life, Keyes engages in a little rhetorical analysis of his own and points out that in the debate over partial-birth abortions, pro-choicers had used the term "medical procedure" as a euphemism for "[sucking] out the brains of a helpless innocent child and [crushing] its head."[17] He goes on to say, "But that which is gruesome and repulsive to us in the facts of its description, ought to be more gruesome and repulsive to us in the truth of its moral principles." Thus, even when Keyes uses graphic language to convey the violence of abortion, he is careful to point out that the real issue is moral principle and not practical application.

That is why Keyes expresses disappointment over the partial-birth abortion debate. Just as antislavery advocates utilized vivid depictions of the horrors of slavery to awaken the consciences of their listeners, they were quick to point out that even under the best of circumstances slavery was wrong. So it is with abortion. Keyes rejoices that many pro-choice advocates were finally faced with a method of abortion they could not support. He is concerned, however, that they missed the more fundamental point:

> But, you know, the gruesomeness of abortion does not lie in its physical brutality only. If you could—and some of them are certainly trying to come up with ways to make it look clean and quick and invisible somehow. I don't care how clean, how quick, how invisible you make it! I don't care how much it can be done in the most secret places! If it violates the open truth, if it violates the standard of right and wrong and

justice on which each and every one of us relies for our claim to human dignity and human rights, then it is wrong! It must be stopped.[18]

Keyes uses the analogy to slavery to draw upon America's theistic roots; to build upon his ethos as a black American; to exploit our cultural reverence for Abraham Lincoln; to call his party back to its origins; to bypass controversy surrounding control of the abortion issue by arguing that the decision of who is human is not properly a human decision; to force his opposition into taking on the role of God if they wish to redefine humanity in anything other than the broadest terms; to provide a compelling vision and model of how American culture can recognize evil and repent, and, to articulate a compelling and clear statement of our nation's moral foundation, one that can be expressed as a fifteen-second sound bite, a format to which our culture is so accustomed. These are the strengths of Keyes' appeal to the analogy between slavery and abortion.

Theism Is Not Sufficient

Having seen some of the benefits of this analogical strategy, what are the problems with Keyes' approach? First, theism is necessary for his position, but it is not sufficient. While the vast majority of Americans routinely identify themselves as theists, their views on God differ dramatically. Keyes must rely on a view of God as a personal Creator who is interested in the affairs of men. If the deistic view of many of the founders is taken seriously, then it may not be significant to humanity whether God created us to be equal since it is now up to us to structure our universe as we see fit. Who cares about God's initial intentions unless He is in some position to enforce those intentions or unless He has designed the universe in such a way that actions contrary to His intentions result in significant harm to violators?

Keyes makes his Judeo-Christian view clear when he discusses the responsibility of citizenship in America:

> Who is the anointed sovereign of the United States of America, anointed by Providence to be the ultimate worldly authority in this land? Who? . . . The people!!! We are anointed to be that authority. Who is the sovereign in America? Who is the king? Who will ulti-

mately stand before God's bar of judgment to answer for how that authority has been used or abused in this country? It will not be Bob Dole and it will not be Bill Clinton and it will not be any other of our chosen ministers of authority. It will be us, answering to God for that part of our citizenship which makes us not the subjects, but the sovereigns of these United States. How we use or abuse that authority which He has granted us.[19]

He relies upon accountability to God to motivate his listeners. God did not simply design the game and then walk away; He is watching, umpiring and will reward us according to our adherence to the rules.[20]

Keyes denies that this emphasis upon God is necessarily a Christian emphasis:

People say I bring religion into it, but if you listen very carefully, what I bring in is the Declaration. And the Declaration does, indeed, refer to the Creator and does require the acknowledgment of a transcendent authority and does draw deeply on Judeo-Christian values and principles. But it does so in a way that is open to all people, not just to those who have a particular religious faith. That's what I think is the strength of this republic, that we have a very broad base in terms of our principles. The Founders were very careful in the way they articulated this in the purest form, as they did in the Declaration. It's a great resource we can draw on as a way of bringing people back to the sense that we have to acknowledge God, but doing it in such a way that you don't necessarily arouse and offend sectarian belief.[21]

A Jewish listener responded to Keyes by asking:

I really admire your passion on the subject of pro-life. And I'm kind of in the middle of all of this. But it seems to me we are so completely torn between the Republicans on the right and the left of this issue, couldn't there [be a position] based on the Jewish Bi-

14

> ble, because there are some leeways, [in which] women
> are allowed to have a choice of having a child up until
> life, which is considered to be three months, couldn't
> somewhere along the line these positions have some
> kind of a meeting place ... on the issue that is not the
> only issue [sic] that matters to our society?[22]

Notice this question points to three issues of importance to Keyes'
position. First, it reduces Keyes' presentation to a passionate expression, a personal statement. Second, it reminds Keyes that there are
other religious traditions that may not see the issue exactly as his does.
Third, it reflects the concern of many voters that there are other issues
of significance, perhaps greater significance, to our society.

Keyes quickly responds to all three issues. First, he reminds his listeners that this position is not a reflection of his personal conviction,
but rather of our nation's founding document, a document that is the
common heritage of this nation. Second, he points out that he has carefully avoided referring to "biblical" principles because these principles,
while consistent with biblical ideals, are an expression of the universal
truth found in the Declaration. Of course, this does not respond directly
to the claim that Jewish Scripture allows for a different standard than he
is articulating. For Keyes, all must bow at the altar of civic religion and
worship a god whose image closely resembles that religious tradition
with which he is most familiar. Finally, he resists the characterization
of this issue as one among many. He states,

> This Republic will not survive if we don't get this issue right. It corrupts everything. It corrupts our heart
> for family life. It corrupts our understanding of freedom, and it corrupts our understanding of responsibility. Without family, without a right understanding
> of freedom, and without a sense of responsibility, this
> Republic can't survive! It can't. We have no choice.
> The money will flow. Things will be here. The science
> will march on. But what we are supposed to represent
> as a people will be gone. What it will be replaced with,
> I don't know.[23]

So our destruction will be moral rather than literal. The American experiment will have failed.

What Keyes rejects is a human foundation for morality. When Keyes asked one young woman where her rights come from, she said they were derived from the Constitution and the Bill of Rights. Keyes pointed out that when the Revolution was fought there was no Constitution and yet the founders claimed to be acting in the name of human rights. Therefore, for Keyes, the fundamental document must be the Declaration. Those rights, however, do not come from the Declaration any more than they do from the Constitution. They simply are recognized in the Declaration as coming from God. Keyes finds this logic inescapable.[24] He concludes this oration to the National Jewish Coalition by saying that the only way to avoid the evil of human arrogation of divine authority "is to remember that there is a God. And we are not Him."[25]

He repeated this theme throughout his campaign. In Louisiana he articulated it as follows:

> So I'll tell you outright. I'll tell you outright. The first principle of a Keyes administration, it will apply in foreign policy, it will apply in domestic policy, it will apply everywhere. There is a God, and we are not him! I will not join the Clinton Democrats who worship government as their god! I will not join the Dole Republicans who worship power as their god! I will not join the Forbes Republicans who worship money as their god! I will stand where the founders of this nation stood, and I will give my respect and allegiance to the creator God who is the ground of justice and who is the ground of all our human rights![26]

The problem for Keyes is that he must play upon the ambiguity of the divine rights giver. This creator God must be the God of civic religion, accessible to people of all faiths, but he must also be someone who rejects interpretations of life that do not begin with conception; that is, someone closely resembling the God of Catholicism.

Keyes Cannot Avoid Defining "Human"

No matter how Keyes tries to finesse the issue, he cannot get around the need for defining who is human. Since we do not have a clear definition from the God of civic religion, we are forced to articulate our essential nature as humans. This means Keyes must violate his own standard against human self-definition. He cannot avoid the quagmire that he must avoid if his argument is to be compelling.

Returning to the slavery analogy, Keyes argues for the broadest possible definition—the position that will result in the least opportunity to deny another person's rights. Therefore, he defines a person as anyone having human parents. His position on this issue is worth stating in full:

> But if human beings can arbitrarily decide who is human and who is not, this command [to respect the rights of all human beings] has no force or effect. Whenever we wished to deny someone's human rights, we could deny that person's humanity and escape the force of the command. So, when whites wished to enslave blacks, they denied their humanity, and so construed the right to hold slaves as a property right. To avoid this absurdity and the injustices that follow from it, we must acknowledge that God has drawn the line that separates human from non-human life, and human beings have no choice but to respect His will. The Declaration of Independence also clearly indicates how we can recognize this line, since it states plainly that we are all created equal, which means that the criterion of our humanity must be such as to provide no grounds for invidious distinctions between one human being and another. Only one criterion meets this requirement; i.e., that we are all of equal parentage. Because our parents were human, we are human. After conception, life in the womb is in this respect no different than life outside the womb. We are, therefore, obliged to treat the human being, once conceived, with the same respect that we demand for ourselves.[27]

This, of course, begs the question and assumes that at the moment of conception a person is created as the offspring of these human parents. Why can't one argue, as many pro-choice advocates do, that human offspring is not present until viability or some other criterion is met?

While his definition has simplicity on its side (it is not dependent upon changing technological standards), it does not avoid the central issue in the abortion debate: who is human? The analogies to slavery and the holocaust may make people wary of definitions requiring people to meet more than the most minimal criterion to be treated as fully human, but it is not apparent that they will accept conception as that criterion.

In "The Role of the Convert in *Eclipse of Reason* and *The Silent Scream*," Robert Branham argues that these pro-life films depict women as "ignorant, irrational, and gullible in order to deny them the ability to choose."[28] Branham claims the films pit men and women against one another in order that men will triumph in the expression of reason and women will be marginalized as decision makers. To his credit, Keyes marginalizes the entire human race as incompetent judges of what constitutes humanity, leaving the decision in the hands of God. The problem I have been laying out is that hearing from God on this issue is no less problematic than on any other issue, and if we are not going to retreat to our subjective worlds of religious conviction, we must find a way of articulating the views of God that will meet with general acceptance. Even in a theistic nation such as the United States, it remains nearly impossible to gain agreement as to what God says on any subject of public significance.

Furthermore, while seeing abortion as a religious issue often sidetracks the discussion into personal views, Keyes is also fighting against the tide of a generation that has grown up with abortion as a legally defined right with moral overtones. That is, Keyes takes that which is predominantly legal in many minds and recasts the issue so that it is predominantly moral. This raises the question: Is Keyes really a politician?

Abortion as a Political Issue

Keyes cannot avoid the political nature of abortion. He is, after all, operating within a political environment and seeking a political affirmation from the nation. One person summed up Keyes' campaign as follows:

> Alan Keyes: A darling of the far Right because of
> his radical-conservative stances on the issues, and
> he's black so supporting him can "prove" that the

Right isn't racist! This is a guy who is proud that he is not a "big tent" Republican, an attitude that is good for cheers at the occasional church picnic rally, but will get him nowhere in politics.[29]

As already discussed, Keyes denies that he is the one who is being divisive, but even so, it is difficult to see how he believes his single-mindedness (reducing everything to morality) will be politically effective. His analogy to the career of Abraham Lincoln is problematic. Politics is a game of compromise, and there does not appear to be much compromise in Keyes' standard.

In his article "On Abortion: A Lincolnian Position," McKenna asks whether pro-lifers have at their disposal a proper rhetorical response to the issue of abortion, one reflective of the political wisdom of Lincoln. McKenna's Lincolnian response is one of permit-restrict-discourage.[30] He suggests the following campaign statement:

According to the Supreme Court, the right to choose abortion is legally protected. That does not change the fact that abortion is morally wrong. It violates the very first of the inalienable rights guaranteed in the Declaration of Independence—the right to life. Even many who would protect and extend the right to choose abortion admit that abortion is wrong, and that killing 1.5 million unborn children a year is, in the understated words of one, "a bad thing." Yet, illogically, they denounce all attempts to restrain it or even to speak out against it. In this campaign I will speak out against it. I will say what is in all our hearts: that abortion is an evil that needs to be restricted and discouraged. If elected, I will not try to abolish an institution that the Supreme Court has ruled to be constitutionally protected, but I will do everything in my power to arrest its further spread and place it where the public can rest in the belief that it is becoming increasingly rare. I take very seriously the imperative, often expressed by abortion supporters, that abortion should be rare. Therefore, if I am elected, I will seek to end all public subsidies for abortion, for abortion advocacy, and for experiments on aborted children. I will support all reasonable abortion restrictions that pass muster with the Supreme Court, and I will encourage those who provide alternatives to abortion. Above all, I mean to treat it as a wrong. I will use the forum provided by my office to speak out against abortion and related practices, such as euthanasia, that violate or undermine the most fundamental of the rights enshrined in this nation's founding charter.[31]

Keyes explicitly rejects this sort of approach as compromising with the moral evil of abortion (just as Garrisonian immediatists argued in response to gradualists such as Lincoln on the issue of slavery). Keyes concedes that if the mother's life is endangered by a pregnancy then abortion is morally justifiable as the ultimate rights of two individuals clash, but he rejects the morality of abortion in cases of rape or incest, two areas of compromise accepted by many in the political arena. He does make two concessions. The first is a political concession. Keyes says he will accept as fellow pro-lifers those who make exceptions for rape and incest, believing an anti-abortion law with these exemptions could be a first step toward the more defensible position. It is difficult to know what the comparable concession would have been with respect to slavery, but in that instance Garrisonian immediatists resisted all compromise.

The second concession is difficult to classify. Keyes says that doctors performing abortions would be prosecuted, but not the women seeking and having abortions. This is another significant disanalogy to slavery. If slavery is banned, then presumably those who would continue to sell or buy slaves would both be prosecuted. Why exempt women from prosecution? Perhaps this position represents political expediency, but if so, Keyes' entire framework of moral consistency begins to collapse. If the answer reflects a view of women as unduly compromised in this situation, as incapable of making rational decisions, then Keyes is open to the charge made by Branham, that this position treats women as ignorant, irrational and gullible. Whatever ground he may have gained by arguing that neither men nor women are the proper decision makers on the issue of who is human would be lost as he reveals himself to have little respect for women's ability to act as fully responsible moral agents.

The Difficulty of Envisioning Victory

While Keyes exhibits the same assurance of victory that character-ized the abolitionists, it is conventional wisdom that abortion is a more complicated issue. A nation convinced of the evil of slavery has been dealing with its guilt for more than a century (despite Lincoln's hopes that the Civil War would be the extent of God's judgment). A nation convinced of the evil of abortion would have to repent not merely the enslavement of millions, but the willful destruction of millions of its own children. This latter would be more psychologically challenging; therefore, resistance to it will understandably be greater.

The issue of states' rights came to the fore in the Civil War and con-tinues to be fought in various legislative skirmishes. As threatening as the national government was to several states, abortion involves the in-dividual and collective rights of women, rights recently acquired after more than a century of political battle, rights that will not easily be sur-rendered.[32]

We have seen the sperm and egg unite, and many are not convinced the result is one of us. While Keyes consistently argues that slavery pic-tured blacks as nonhuman, it is more accurate to say that most whites recognized blacks as inferior humans. The recognition of humanity is more difficult in the case of abortion, particularly early-term abortions. Thus, Keyes' optimism about an imminent pro-life victory appears a bit naive.

He uses the analogy to slavery to enhance his argument against abor-tion, but in the end there are significant problems with this analogy, problems one is likely to overlook if already convinced, problems that will appear insurmountable if one is not. Keyes uses the political arena to agitate against abortion. Perhaps he will learn from his own analogy and the experiences of abolitionists, seeing that a position of uncompro-mising principle is best articulated from within the community at large, but outside the moral ambiguity and compromise of political games-manship.[33]

Endnotes

1. See William B. Prendergast, "Interpreting the Catholic Vote in 1992," *America* (Octo-ber 16, 1993): 15-20.

2. Of course, they are still far apart on issues such as gambling. See Darrell Turner, "Religion, Politics Make Fickle Bedfellows," *National Catholic Reporter* (October 18, 1996; Internet edition).

3. Speech delivered to Black Americans for Life in Indianapolis, Indiana, November 4, 1995. Available online at http://www.sandh.com/keyes/speeches.html.

4. Interview with Wolf Blitzer on "Inside Politics," August 27, 1995.

5. Speech delivered at the Delaware State Republican Dinner, April 8, 1995.

6. George McKenna, "On Abortion: A Lincolnian Position," *The Atlantic Monthly* (September 1995; Internet edition).

7. Ibid.

8. Speech delivered to GOPAC in Washington, D.C., May 1, 1995.

9. Aileen S. Kraditor, *Means and Ends in American Abolitionism: Garrison and His Critics on Strategy and Tactics, 1834-1850* (1969; reprint, Chicago: Ivan R. Dee, Inc., 1989), 28-29.

10. Ibid., 28.

11. Blitzer interview.

12. Letter to David Quackenbush, June 30, 1995. This letter was included with Keyes' position paper on abortion (see http://www.sandh.com/keyes/index.html).

13. Speech delivered at a Republican gathering in New Hampshire, February 2, 1995. It is virtually identical to the transcript of the speech aired on "Focus on the Family" on February 22, 1995, yet the transcript for this show lists the date of delivery as February 19, 1995.

14. Ibid.

15. Black Americans for Life speech.

16. Ibid.

17. Ibid.

18. Speech delivered at an Operation Rescue rally in Lemon Grove, California, August 13, 1996.

19. Speech delivered at the Wanderer Forum, October 12, 1996.

20. Keyes also shifts the locus of authority and responsibility from the government to the governed, reminiscent of Lincoln's "government of the people, by the people, for the people." Of course, this emphasis may backfire on Christian pro-lifers (who are commanded by Scripture to obey those in authority), if a majority of Americans support legalized abortion.

21. Interview with Rush Limbaugh, October 1995.

22. Speech delivered to the National Jewish Coalition, November 28, 1995.

23. Ibid.

24. Ibid.

25. Ibid.

26. Speech delivered at the Louisiana Republican Convention, January 27, 1996.

27. Alan Keyes, "Alan Keyes: On Abortion and Euthanasia." Available: http://sandh.com/keyes/abortion.html. This quotation comes from Keyes' 1996 presidential campaign position paper on abortion and euthanasia.

28. Robert Branham, "The Role of the Convert in *Eclipse of Reason* and *The Silent Scream*," *Quarterly Journal of Speech* 77 (1991): 423.

29. This quotation comes from a web page entitled, "Optimism for 1996 . . . Clinton/Gore: Four More!" Available: http://www.cjnetworks.com/~cubsfan/96.html. This page evaluates briefly the chances of the 1996 Republican presidential candidates against incumbent Bill Clinton.

30. McKenna also refers to the strategy as "grudgingly tolerate-restrict-discourage" and "tolerate-restrict-discourage."

31. Ibid.

32. Of course, one pro-life argument is that those who use abortion for sex selection almost always eliminate female offspring. In such a case, the right to abortion perpetuates the cultural tendency to denigrate female worth.

23. While this paper focuses on the 1996 presidential campaign, Keyes' bid in 2000 reiterated the same themes: the significance of the Declaration of Independence with its vision of human dignity, as well as the contention that abortion today is analogous to American slavery.

Stewardship and the Kingdom of God

Ronald Walborn and Frank Chan

There is a crisis in Christianity today. Many churches and denominations are struggling to reach their financial goals and fund their visions. We in The Christian and Missionary Alliance are no strangers to this struggle. But the crisis we face is not primarily a struggle of stewardship. It is a crisis of discipleship. Certainly, stewardship flows out of this broader category of discipleship, but the central issue is the totality of what it means to be a follower of Jesus in the twenty-first century.

The church in North America has tragically and unknowingly reduced following Jesus to a series of creeds to believe and a group of prayers to be prayed. Lost in our evangelism is the radical call to leave the kingdom of this world and come under the rule and reign of God. Our call to become citizens of the kingdom of God has made few demands on previous worldly allegiances. We have produced a generation of disciples who do not mind taking up their cross so long as it is not too heavy, fits into their schedule and does not conflict with their lifestyle. We have preached a bloodless cross that has robbed Christianity of its power and has turned the biblical teaching of stewardship into a task most preachers would rather avoid.

The time has come for The Christian and Missionary Alliance to revisit the meaning of biblical stewardship, to relearn the principles that guide our earning, spending, saving and giving, and to recommit ourselves as men and women devoted to radical obedience. Toward this goal, as with all areas of daily discipleship, we must remind ourselves of the central message of our Lord Jesus Christ.

"The kingdom of God is near." What did Jesus mean when he made that declaration in Mark 1:15? What relationship does it have to a biblical theology of stewardship? Jesus' bold proclamation directly addressed humanity's central problem: its fallenness. The fall of man resulted in a hostile takeover of this planet. The ensuing alienation between man and God and between man and his fellowman horrifically displayed the rule and reign of evil on this earth. Jesus' mission was to reestablish the redemptive beachhead of the rule and reign of God.

Dallas Willard paraphrases Mark 1:15 to convey this awesome truth: "Jesus then came into Galilee announcing the good news from God. 'All the preliminaries have been taken care of,' He said, 'and the rule of God is now accessible to everyone. Review your plans for living and base your life on this remarkable new opportunity.' "[1] In other words, Jesus was making available a whole new economy under which we may live. "Here it is," declares Jesus. "The kingdom of God is within your reach. God's rule and reign is available to all who will receive it."

Matthew's record of this announcement includes the well-known directive, "Repent, for the kingdom of heaven is near" (Matthew 4:17). Inherent in this call is the requirement to turn from the direction in which one is heading and to move into a whole new reality. Repentance (Greek: *metanoeo*) means to change one's mind or purpose.[2] "Change your life. God's kingdom is here," is how Eugene Peterson renders this verse in *The Message*. He captures the heart of Jesus' message. You can enter into the kingdom of God only if you are willing to let go of the "apparent" control you have over your own life. A kingdom proclamation that neglects the call to reconsider and repent of previous values and priorities brings forth lifestyles that fall short of what Jesus sought.

Some have suggested that this kingdom reality was and is for a future time, that the kingdom is not available now, but someday will be.[3] While there are certainly elements of the kingdom that we have yet to experience, Jesus appears to have been inviting His listeners to enter into something immediately accessible. The perfect tense of *eggiken*, usually translated "is at hand" or "has drawn nigh" (Matthew 3:2; 4:17; 10:7; Mark 1:15), indicates that the "coming" is a past action with present results.[4] Jesus proclaimed that the rule and reign of God, though not yet fully consummated, is available now.[5]

If Jesus' call to the kingdom was really a call to receive the rule and reign of God, it is obvious that the one responding to this call cannot remain the same. Clearly falling under God's lordship would be the use of his or her money, gifts, abilities and all resources. We who enter the kingdom, therefore, undergo a radical change. We serve a new Master, and everything we have belongs to Him (Psalm 24:1). If God owns our hearts, He will most certainly have our wallets as well.

Any discussion of stewardship must therefore begin with a healthy understanding of kingdom discipleship. We must resist our tendency to limit our concept of stewardship to matters of money and finance, because biblical stewardship encompasses far more: it means coming fully under the reign of God in every area of our lives. A.B. Simpson, in his article, "The Grace of Giving," describes this wonderful connection between kingdom discipleship and stewardship:

When we began our mission on Tremont Street in Boston, I remember taking up an offering for it at an afternoon meeting in the city. The largest gift was $25—a substantial sum at that time. I was curious as to who the "$25 person" was. At the close of the meeting I was introduced to him—a poor shoemaker who had a small shop. When I spoke to him about his generous gift he said, "If you only knew what the Lord has given me, you would not wonder at all." Subsequently I became better acquainted with the man. Every time I went to Boston, there he was, shouting his hallelujahs. He was converted many years before, but he could get no joy. He was hungry for more of God's presence. He sought a deeper experience with God, but the members of the church he attended told him his quest was nonsense. "You must be contented to sin like the rest of us," they advised. The man backslid and for several years he kept a saloon in Boston. But his heart hunger would not go away. One Thursday afternoon he stumbled into our Alliance meeting in Boston and he heard people talking about the riches of Christ's grace. Before the afternoon was over, he had received the Holy Spirit. He went home to pitch his whiskey into the sea. He closed his saloon and returned to making shoes for a living. There in his little shop he preached the gospel all day long to the customers. And that was the man who gave $25. It was a gift that God enabled and that God impelled by the fullness of the Holy Spirit and the overflow of His grace.[6]

The distinguishing factor of this man's giving was his heart. Though he had been a Christian for years, he hungered insatiably for more of God's presence. He finally experienced it only after he was willing to abandon his idols and return to the simplicity of pure devotion to Jesus. Monetarily he made little as a shoemaker, but receiving wholeheartedly from the One who owns it all made him rich indeed. As a result, his desire was both to tell and to give. He didn't just preach about God's grace. He lived it. People who understand what they have in the kingdom of our Lord give generously and joyfully. People who have not been so taught will not.

This conviction, we believe, serves as the starting point for the proper stewardship of all that we possess. The principles that we present and the issues we address in the pages that follow cannot be understood without the Lordship of Christ as their true foundation.[7] Because of the limited scope of our discussion, we cannot address every point of Scripture and every matter of concern.[8] Nevertheless, our hope is that this paper will serve as a concise summary of what every pastor, elder and layperson should know about biblical stewardship.

I. Stewardship Defined

Merriam-Webster's Collegiate Dictionary defines a steward as "one employed in a large household or estate to manage domestic concerns (as the supervision of servants, collection of rents, and keeping of accounts)."[9] In short, a steward is a person who takes care of someone else's property. There are several examples in the Old Testament, where they are described simply as those "over the household" (Hebrew: *al-habbayit*, e.g., 1 Kings 4:6, 16:9, Isaiah 36:3 NASB), as well as in the New Testament, where they are called managers or stewards (Greek: *oikonomoi*, e.g., Luke 12:42; 16:1). We should also mention Paul's illustration in Galatians 3:24 likening the Old Testament law to a household slave put in charge of children (Greek: *paidagogos*). Perhaps the most vivid biblical story illustrating stewardship is Joseph, the manager of Potiphar's house (Genesis 39:4-6).[10] While these passages offer helpful illustrations of the occupation of stewardship, the heart of the Bible's teaching on stewardship as a point of discipleship goes much deeper.

A. The Concept of Stewardship in the Old Testament

The Hebrew concept of stewardship begins and ends with God. God is the creator and possessor of all things. Human beings who possess God's creation do so only as God graciously delegates. This idea may be traced throughout the entire Old Testament. In Genesis 1 and 2, when God grants Adam and Eve dominion over the creation, He is asking them to rule *on His behalf*. The responsibilities of naming the animals, filling and subduing the earth show that they are being given an ambassadorial reign as God's vice-regents. However, there is never any doubt as to who is the true Sovereign. The judgment Adam and Eve undergo after they chose to go their own way and come out from under the rule and reign of God in Genesis 3 shows that they were held accountable by the Lord. Stewardship responsibility in the kingdom of God was established from the beginning.

In Genesis 14, when Melchizedek brings out the bread and the wine and blesses Abram, the first words out of his mouth are, "Blessed be Abram by God Most High, Possessor (Hebrew: *qanah*) of heaven and earth" (14:19, NASB). Verse 20 records the first tithe in Scripture: "And he gave him a tenth of all." Two verses later Abram raises his hand and makes Melchizedek's blessing personal, in essence declaring, "Lord God Most High, everything I have belongs to You." It is fitting that this tithe is framed by the bold declaration that the Lord is the creator and possessor of all things.

In Deuteronomy, when the Israelites were poised to move into the Promised Land, they were carefully instructed to remember that the land truly belonged to God. They were, at best, temporary tenants. The land was God's gift and their inheritance from Him (Deuteronomy 25:19). They could not do anything they pleased with it. Rather, they were to be good stewards of the resources God had entrusted to them.

This notion was behind many of the laws concerning their use of the land. Two examples are worth noting here. First, God commanded that His land was to lie fallow every seventh year to receive a Sabbath rest from planting and harvest. "For six years you are to sow your fields and harvest the crops, but during the seventh year let the land lie unplowed and unused. Then the poor among your people may get food from it, and the wild animals may eat what they leave. Do the same with your vineyard and your olive grove" (Exodus 23:10-11). The crops from preceding years were promised to be sufficient to carry them through the

Sabbath year of rest. Through this law, God was teaching His people that He was to be their source of sustenance, that they should trust in His ability to provide for them more than in their ability to provide for themselves. Over the years, the people of Israel sadly ignored this Sabbatical year law. When the Chronicler looked back on the fall of Jerusalem in 586 BC, he interpreted the people's downfall and the Babylonian captivity in terms of their inability to trust and obey God in this very matter: "He carried into exile to Babylon the remnant. . . . The land enjoyed its sabbath rests" (2 Chronicles 36:20-21).

Second, the concepts of stewardship underlay laws concerning the Year of Jubilee. Every fiftieth year was consecrated as a fresh start throughout the land (Leviticus 25:8-54). Outcasts and prodigals were to return home. Debts were to be forgiven. Land was to be returned to the original owners. Why was this done? The Lord declared that the land rightfully belonged to Him, and no one but He could claim absolute ownership of it. "The land must not be sold permanently, because the land is mine and you are but aliens and my tenants" (25:23).

Thus, the covenant people of God in the Old Testament had a very clear understanding of the concept of stewardship. Even their songs of worship contained references and reminders to this important spiritual principle. "The earth is the LORD's and everything in it, the world, and all who live in it; for he founded it . . ." (Psalm 24:1-2). Again, through the Psalmist, God asserts, "For every animal of the forest is mine, and the cattle on a thousand hills. I know every bird in the mountains, and the creatures of the field are mine. If I were hungry I would not tell you, for the world is mine, and all that is in it" (50:10-12).

This theology of God's ownership also undergirds the Israelite practice of tithes and offerings. There are three different tithes mentioned in the Old Testament: a tithe for the Levites (Numbers 18:21-24), a celebration tithe of agricultural products (Deuteronomy 12:6-7; 14:22-26), and a charity tithe (14:28-29).[11] Regardless of the earthly purpose, the core purpose of these offerings was always to be the heart worship of the God who was the owner and giver of everything. We will address this concept of the spirit of the tithe more fully in another section. For the moment, we might say that this heart worship is beautifully illustrated in the Chronicler's description of the gifts the people of Israel brought for the building of the temple. "The people rejoiced at the willing response of their leaders, for they had given freely and wholeheartedly to the LORD" (1 Chronicles 29:9). David, overwhelmed by this outpouring of generosity, breaks into praise, saying,

> But who am I, and who are my people, that we should be able to give as generously as this? Everything comes from you, and we have given you only what comes from your hand. . . . I know, my God, that you test the heart and are pleased with integrity. All these things have I given willingly and with honest intent. And now I have seen with joy how willingly your people who are here have given to you. O LORD, God of our fathers Abraham, Isaac and Israel, keep this desire in the hearts of your people forever. (29:14, 17-18)

The Old Testament teaching on stewardship may be summarized in three principles: 1) God is the owner of everything; 2) God's covenant people are held responsible for their management of God's resources; 3) Giving is a worshipful response to God's ownership of all things.

B. The Concept of Stewardship in the New Testament

> The Lord answered, "Who then is the faithful and wise manager, whom the master puts in charge of his servants to give them their food allowance at the proper time? It will be good for that servant whom the master finds doing so when he returns. I tell you the truth, he will put him in charge of all his possessions. But suppose the servant says to himself, 'My master is taking a long time in coming,' and he then begins to beat the menservants and maidservants and to eat and drink and get drunk. The master of that servant will come on a day when he does not expect him and at an hour he is not aware of. He will cut him to pieces and assign him a place with the unbelievers.
>
> "That servant who knows his master's will and does not get ready or does not do what his master wants will be beaten with many blows. But the one who does not know and does things deserving punishment will be beaten with few blows. From everyone who has been given much, much will be demanded; and from the

one who has been entrusted with much, much more
will be asked." (Luke 12:42-48)

Jesus' parable of the faithful and unfaithful servants continues the theology of God's ownership found in the Old Testament. The master in the parable who is "coming" and entrusts his possessions to his servants would have been recognized by Jewish hearers as God, whom the prophets said would "come" on the Day of the Lord.

For many first-century Palestinian Jews, this "coming" meant the arrival of a political messiah who would deliver them from the rule of the Roman Empire. Their expectancy that Jesus would usher in the kingdom of God was high.[12] However, Jesus' introduction to this parable reinterprets this expected Day of the Lord as the day of his own Second Coming: "You too, be ready; for the Son of Man is coming at an hour that you do not expect" (Luke 12:40, NASB).[13] The effect of this interpretive move had profound implications for Christian stewardship. In effect, Jesus was teaching them not only that the fullness of the kingdom of God was to be delayed, but that in the meantime, while the kingdom is "now" and "not yet," they must live a life of faithful stewardship.

The word "manager" (Greek: *oikonomos*) in Luke 12:42 appears frequently in Greek literature, in both literary works (e.g., Philo and Josephus) and nonliterary works (receipts, lease agreements, etc., on Greek papyri).[14] It referred to managers of payable accounts (e.g., Luke 16:1-8) as well as city treasurers (e.g. Erastus in Romans 16:23). Yet common to all of them was that they were responsible for property that wasn't theirs and were accountable for what they did with it. By analogy, Jesus' parable calls God's people to live as responsible and accountable stewards of all that God has entrusted to them.

A final word about the "coming" of the Master: the time period envisioned for the reward (Luke 12:44) and punishment (12:46) of the stewards is clearly the *parousia*, when the kingdom of God is consummated. But the eschatology of the New Testament is a "realized" eschatology. The heart of Jesus' message was that end-time realities (healing, defeat of demons, the presence of God in the Holy Spirit, the forgiveness of sins, etc.) are present in token form now. Even though the faithful may anticipate heavenly rewards (being put in charge of *everything* the master owns, 12:44) and the unfaithful punishment in hell (being cut into pieces, 12:46), there is no reason why these future outcomes cannot be experienced on a smaller scale on earth now. We must be open to the possibility that people within God's kingdom, both the true and the false (cf. Matthew 13:24-29; 36-43; 47-50), may undergo *in this life* the material blessing and material curse (!) of God.

As we move beyond this parable to the rest of the New Testament, it becomes clear that our stewardship consists in more than just material things. In First Corinthians 4:1 (NASB), Paul says Christian workers are stewards (plural: *oikonomoi*) of "the mysteries of God." Paul is probably referring to the gospel, the mystery of "the manifold wisdom of God," that the Church has been entrusted to make known (Ephesians 3:9-10). Related to this is his use of the word "stewardship" (*oikonomia*) to describe his preaching of the gospel (1 Corinthians 9:16-17). In Titus 1:7, while listing the qualifications for elders, Paul describes the overseer as God's "steward" (*oikonomos*). Paul is teaching that church leaders who are entrusted with God's church are accountable to God for their oversight. Finally, First Peter 4:10 (NASB) says, "As each one has received a special gift, employ it serving one another, as good stewards (*oikonomoi*) of the manifold grace of God." Peter then goes on to list speaking and serving gifts as the domain of our stewardship (4:11). The gospel, our churches, the gifts of the Holy Spirit—none of these wonderful blessings belong to us. We are the gracious recipients of the good things of God. Therefore, we are responsible for their use on this earth, and we will ultimately be held accountable for our faithfulness with them (Matthew 16:27; Romans 14:10-12; 1 Corinthians 3:10-15; 2 Corinthians 5:10).

Unfortunately, this concept of stewardship may be more palatable when it remains a mere theological principle than when it becomes a call to practical Christian living. It is not difficult to accept Christian stewardship in the abstract, but we are slow to embrace it when it impinges upon tangible realities. "Yes, I know God owns everything, but why is it so hard for me to surrender my children into His care when they want to pursue missions?" If we are responsible for the use of our gifts and abilities, why do we conduct our ministries more out of our own convenience than out of a sense of God's calling? Why do we look down upon sacrificial giving as a legalistic practice done only in those "radical" churches? These questions point to matters of the heart and challenge us in our willingness, or perhaps unwillingness, to obey. We each must pause and consider our ways (Haggai 1:7), allowing the Spirit to convict, that we might learn how and when we give into the false assumption that we, and not God, are true owners of what we have. It is with this spirit that we offer these seven practical principles that build upon the biblical material we've covered.

C. Principles of Stewardship

1. *Good stewardship begins with the recognition that God is the owner of all things.* The prayer of David quoted earlier summarizes beautifully the foundational idea of stewardship: "Everything comes from you" (1 Chronicles 29:14). The plea of the preacher to "give God ownership of your life" is based on a false premise. Our lives and everything we have is not ours to give. We cannot "give" God ownership of our material goods. He already owns it all. We can only recognize and submit to His ownership.

In addition to the parable of the faithful and unfaithful servants (Luke 12:42-48), there are other stewardship parables, most notably the parable of the unjust steward (Luke 16:1-13) and the parable of the talents (Matthew 25:14-20 and Luke 19:12-27). Taking these three parables together, we can set forth the next three principles about our stewardship before God.

2. *As stewards, we are entrusted with goods to care for as part of kingdom discipleship until the return of the Master, Jesus Christ.* A few points may be drawn from the Parable of the Talents concerning the ways in which God entrusts His "goods" to us. First, the servants received different amounts. In the same way, not all of us are entrusted by God with the same things—some receive greater responsibilities, some lesser. Second, Matthew's version tells us that the master distributed the talents according to the servants' own abilities (Matthew 25:15). We can trust that God in His providence puts into our hands only what we can aptly handle. Third, the master expected an increase. Judgment came to the third servant for failing even to bring interest (Luke 19:23; Matthew 25:27). Likewise, God expects us to bear fruit in His kingdom. Finally, in Matthew's version, the master is equally pleased with the second servant who yielded two talents as he is with the first who yielded five talents. We should not look to how God has dealt with others to evaluate how He deals with us. He is mainly concerned with our being faithful (Luke 12:42) with what we have been given.

3. *Earthly resources can be used for eternal purposes.* In Jesus' surprising parable of the shrewd manager (Luke 16), one of the key lessons taught

is that worldly wealth can have eternal value. Jesus warned that money has the potential of becoming a controlling influence in our lives (16:13), and it had become so in the lives of the Pharisees (16:14). Their earthly view of money caused them to place a wrong value on it (16:15). In contrast, we are to view money as a tool God can use to accomplish eternal work. Wise is the person who uses his earthly resources so that he may someday enjoy eternal returns on his investment (16:9). Certainly the New Testament promise can be applied to those who give financially to God's work, "God is not unjust; he will not forget your work and the love you have shown him as you have helped his people and continue to help them" (Hebrews 6:10).

4. *Our stewardship must not serve our own purposes, but the purpose of the Master, Jesus Christ.* The third servant in the parable of the talents did what appeared right in his own eyes but was judged for not obeying the will of the master. Indeed, the greatest punishment in the parable of the faithful and unfaithful servants comes to the servant who knew the master's will and did not do it (Luke 12:47). By contrast, the parable of the servant in Luke 17:7-10 reminds us of the primacy of obedience in the master-servant relationship. Even if we do everything God has asked us to do, we should remember that obedience is only a minimum expectation. We are in line for no special reward. We are simply serving our Master.

5. *As stewards, we need a balanced picture of hardship.* An important part of understanding stewardship is understanding God's view of hardship. For most Americans, it is easy to experience ongoing lifestyle inflation. This means that every year the bar is raised as to what constitutes normal living. Yesterday's want becomes today's need. As this occurs, we can take on a skewed view of hardship. Things that would have been considered routine aspects of life may now be considered hardship. A subtle shift can then occur where we believe that such hardship could not be a part of God's will. We begin to say, "That couldn't be God's will," simply because it is hard. But in fact, God has often called His people to hardship. There are several occurrences in the Gospels where Jesus addresses the issue of hardship (Matthew 8:19-22, 10:22; Mark 10:45).

This is not to say that just because it is hard means that it is what God wants. A balanced view of hardship means that God's call on our lives should not be determined by what is most comfortable or most difficult. This principle is particularly important in an era of high debt. Minimizing debt, giving sacrificially, moving in new ministry directions may require a simpler lifestyle. For some, this may be an easy adjustment. For many others, however, this may involve significant hardship. If our picture of hardship is skewed, we may end up dismissing such important steps because we are adverse to hardship.

6. *We will be held accountable for our stewardship.* In all three stewardship parables, there is a moment of reckoning. The unjust steward faces it at the beginning of the story when he is fired. The stewards in the parable of the faithful and unfaithful servants and the parable of the talents face it at the end, when they are rewarded and punished. The New Testament reminds us of the Christian's day of reckoning before the Judgment Seat of Christ, sometimes referred to as the "Bema Seat" (2 Corinthians 5:10). Salvation is a free gift given by God's grace (Ephesians 2:8-9), yet each of us will still be judged by Christ to determine our rewards for how we have lived. Our redemption does not remove us from responsibility and accountability before God. The covenant people of God will one day give an account for their stewardship (Matthew 16:27; 1 Corinthians 3:10-15). Paul tells the Romans that "each of us will give an account of himself to God" (Romans 14:12). This means that we will have to give an explanation for what we did and why we did it. It will not only be an evaluation of deed, but also an evaluation of the heart. The judgment for poor stewardship will not result in the loss of salvation, but there will still be loss: "If what he has built survives, he will receive his reward. If it is burned up, he will suffer loss; he himself will be saved, but only as one escaping through the flames" (1 Corinthians 3:14-15). To put it bluntly, "He will be saved, but with the smell of smoke all over him."

7. *Our stewardship embraces both the spiritual and the material.* We have already mentioned the New Testament passages that use the word *oikonomos* or *oikonomia* to describe the items over which Christians are stewards (the church, the gospel, spiritual gifts). There are other passages that do not contain these key words but still set forth items that properly fall under our stewardship care. The use of time and opportunities to minister (Ephesians 5:15-16) certainly must be governed with wise stewardship. Since our physical bodies are temples of the Holy Spirit (1 Corinthians 6:19), our care of them is also a stewardship. Finally, the Lord would be well pleased if the stewardship of our homes

included the welcoming of others in hospitality (Hebrews 13:2, 1 Peter 4:9).

II. Practical Directives on Four Related Issues

A. Spiritual Warfare

Why are Christians resistant to the issues of stewardship? Why do we not live as Jesus taught us to live? Two possible answers to these questions are hard-heartedness (we know what God says and we don't care) and ignorance (we don't know because we haven't been taught). Certainly these are issues that need to be addressed, but could it be we are overlooking a further possible cause?

In our Western sophistication we have often neglected the influence of the spirit-realm. We believe Jesus made reference to the presence of spiritual warfare in relation to stewardship in Matthew 6:19-24:

> Do not store up for yourselves treasures on earth, where moth and rust destroy, and where thieves break in and steal. But store up for yourselves treasures in heaven, where moth and rust do not destroy, and where thieves do not break in and steal. For where your treasure is, there your heart will be also.
>
> The eye is the lamp of the body. If your eyes are good, your whole body will be full of light. But if your eyes are bad, your whole body will be full of darkness. If then the light within you is darkness, how great is that darkness!
>
> No one can serve two masters. Either he will hate the one and love the other, or he will be devoted to the one and despise the other. You cannot serve both God and Money.

Note in this passage the strongly worded statement that one cannot serve two masters (*kurios* = Lord). In particular, these two masters, God and Money (6:24), are diametrically opposed and cannot coexist. The impossibility of serving both is expressed well by the metaphor of servitude. There is no such thing as a slave's "part-time" obligation to his owner. A master's control over his slave was total and complete. One writer puts the conflicting demands of the two "masters" this way:

The one commands us to walk by faith and the other commands we walk by sight. The one calls us to be humble and the other to be proud. The one to set our minds on things above and the other to set them on things below. One calls us to love light, the other to love darkness. The one tells us to look toward things unseen and eternal and the other to look at things seen and temporal.[15]

Could it be that Jesus' slave imagery is a clue that He views a believer's allegiance to money as a form of spiritual bondage? Certainly those who have ministered to parishioners who live under the rule of materialism, workaholism, gambling and the bitter fear of losing what they have, know that there is an oppressive and binding nature to these sins. Jesus' personification of "Money" or "Mammon" (Greek: *mamonas*, derived from Aramaic) may be more than a mere literary device. We must be open to the possibility that He is speaking of Mammon as a demonic spirit, a rival god, a ruling principality.

Many today indeed take the word "Mammon" in Matthew 6:24 this way. Richard Foster, in his book, *Money, Sex and Power*, says Mammon is a spiritual power that seeks to dominate our lives.[16] One pastor has suggested that the root of this word comes from a mining term meaning to dig in the earth; to find one's sustenance in the ground. The picture is that of a man digging and clawing at the earth, constantly looking downward, drawing his life not from above, but from the world below.[17] Though a word's meaning can never be derived from its etymology, we nevertheless have a convenient picture illustrating the spiritual bondage of a person for whom wealth has become a God-substitute. Those ruled by Mammon suffer under the satanic lie that man-made things (employers, the stock market, one's own toil, even luck) are their provider instead of God, their true Provider.

There is certainly a spirit of Mammon that is active in the United States of America. Christians must therefore be alert and ready to employ the weapons of spiritual warfare, not only in extraordinary situations involving the occult and demonic manifestations, but also in the ordinary world of wage earning, bill paying and tithing. A life of good Christian stewardship is a spiritual battle that must be waged and won.

There are many different understandings of how to go about spiritual warfare. Some of these are extremely controversial. Here is a method of spiritual warfare that will be widely accepted. It is also a good course of action even if the manifestation is not primarily demonic. Whatever spirit appears to be manifesting—pride, greed or anger for example—live out the opposite spirit. In Proverbs 15:1 we read, "A gentle answer turns away wrath." When a person is exhibiting anger or wrath, the best course of action is to respond with the opposite spirit—gentleness. Jesus instructed us to respond to cursing with blessing and to pray for those who were mistreating us (Luke 6:28).

Where a spirit of pride has taken over, nothing will expose it like a spirit of humility. A missionary with Youth With A Mission tells of an outreach in a large South American city. During the first few days they had little success in their evangelism. Several of the team members had been verbally abused, and all of them had been openly mocked. No one would even take the tracts the street teams were trying to hand out.

They decided to fast and pray for a day to see if they could discern what was going on in the realm of the spirit. Several of the team members sensed that there was a strong spirit of pride over the city that needed to be broken before the gospel could go forth. After further prayer, they decided to respond with symbolic acts of humility throughout the city. Team members scattered and knelt on street corners to pray for the people of the city. They began to offer themselves for humble acts of service throughout the business district. Some voluntarily cleaned filthy bathrooms and emptied trash for shops and restaurants.

Within twenty-four hours something dramatic and supernatural began to take place. People began to listen when the team shared their faith. They took their tracts and actually read them. Team members began to ask people if they could pray for them, and many graciously received Christ in the middle of crowded sidewalks. Prior to their acts of humility, no one had received Christ. By the end of the week, more than 300 people had said, "Yes," to Jesus, praying to be born again with the team members.[18]

Was there really a demonic spirit of pride over that city? We do not know. But whether a stronghold is rooted in the demonic or the sin-hardened heart of people, living out the opposite spirit can bring the light and freedom of God.

This directly relates to the spirit of Mammon in our culture. Whether this is demonic or not, our response should be the same—practice the opposite spirit by the grace of God. Where there is greed, let generosity abound. Where materialism and worldly wealth have become all important, let the church of Jesus Christ live by a different economy—one ruled by the King of love and generosity, Jesus Christ. "For you know the grace of our Lord Jesus Christ, that though he was rich, yet for your sakes he became poor, so that you through his poverty might become rich" (2 Corinthians 8:9).

This verse describes the ultimate generosity of the God-Man Christ Jesus, "Who, being in very nature God, did not consider equality with God something to be grasped, but made himself nothing, taking the very nature of a servant, being made in human likeness" (Philippians 2:6-7). Jesus freely gave of Himself and generously laid aside His rights and privileges that we could be free. Jesus became poor for us, so that we through His poverty might become rich. This is the ultimate act of generosity. Jesus' intention was that His disciples would follow His example.

B. The Health and Wealth Gospel

Does God promise to bless His children with health and wealth? Many of us have encountered preachers and writers in the health/wealth/prosperity movement who have led many to believe that the answer is a resounding, "Yes."[19] We love these Christian brothers and sisters like family, but we believe they are in error in some significant areas.

Before we speak words of correction, allow us to offer a word of caution to those, including ourselves, who are prone to harshly denouncing the faith movement. First, as we disagree we must refrain from being censorious and judgmental. If, in our effort to speak the truth, we hurt and slander, we not only lose the opportunity for godly correction, but we invite God's discipline on our own heads.

Second, as we bring correction we must be careful not to cast away God's truth in the process. A parallel situation will illustrate what we mean. For the past thirty years God has been restoring the use of spiritual gifts to the church, particularly the so-called "miraculous" ones (e.g. healing, prophecy, etc.). It has been said concerning the gifts, "Disuse is not the answer to misuse, but rather right use is the answer to misuse." In the same way, we must be careful not to abandon some of the examples in Scripture about God's material blessing.

With these cautions in mind, we may identify a few extremes to which the health-and-wealth gospel has fallen prey. First, we must reject as unbiblical the suggestion that God has set up universal laws of prosperity that govern the cosmos, put into operation by faith and positive confession (name it and claim it).[20] Second, we must reject as unbiblical the claim that God wants to meet not only the believer's every need but to grant every desire as well ("King's kids ought to ride in Rolls Royces").[21] Finally, we must reject as unbiblical the claim that Jesus died to redeem man from poverty, and that a believer who is poor has dishonored God because he has failed to appropriate the deliverance from poverty provided in the Atonement.[22]

On the other hand, our misgivings about the health-and-wealth gospel must not lead us to devalue scriptural passages that show that God's desire is to bless and even prosper His children. The Old Testament describes many examples of people whom God materially blessed: Abraham (Genesis 13:2,6), Isaac (26:13-14), Jacob (32:9-12), Job (Job 1:3; 42:10) and Solomon (1 Kings 3:13). According to Deuteronomy, God used prosperity to confirm His covenant with Israel and to teach the nations to fear them (8:18; 28:8-10). The familiar verse, "This is the day the LORD has made" (Psalm 118:24) is followed by a less familiar plea for success: "O LORD, do save, we beseech Thee; O LORD, we beseech Thee, do send prosperity!" (118:25, NASB).

Ecclesiastes sanctions satisfaction from food and drink by affirming that such enjoyment is not sinful, but a gift from God (2:24-25). The New Testament, while it focuses less on material blessings and more on spiritual blessings, nevertheless affirms that we should enjoy the material things God gives us. The early Christians "partook of food with glad and generous hearts, praising God" (Acts 2:46-47, RSV). Paul, in spite of his warnings about riches, tells Timothy that even wealthy people should set their hopes on God "who richly furnishes us with everything to enjoy" (1 Timothy 6:17, RSV).

Yet this teaching on God's desire to bless stands in tension with other passages, especially in the New Testament, that warn against riches. Jesus condemned the rich fool (Luke 12:13-20) and warned about how hard it is for a rich man to enter into the kingdom of God (18:24-25). How do we reconcile the positive and negative teachings on wealth? The best way is still to affirm that wealth is not evil in and of itself. It is our attitude toward wealth, namely our desire for it, that can make its possession evil (1 Timothy 6:9-10).

But if, as we said earlier, God's desire is to bless, what should we make of believers who are in poverty? We must first affirm, against the health-and-wealth gospel, that there is no shame in being poor. Jesus

Himself had "nowhere to lay his head" (Luke 9:58, RSV). Paul described himself as "ill-clad" and "homeless" (1 Corinthians 4:11). Jesus pronounced a blessing on the poor: "Blessed are you who are poor, for yours is the kingdom of God" (Luke 6:20, RSV). James tells us that God has "chosen those who are poor" to be rich in faith (James 2:5). God is in no way dishonored by believers who have little or no possessions.

On the other hand, we must affirm that material poverty is part of the *curse* of our fallen world. There are, of course, persons who choose a simple lifestyle out of obedience to the call of God, but we are not addressing their situation. We are addressing those believers who have been "taken by" poverty and who have not chosen it. It is time to reconsider writers like Ron Sider, who, while acknowledging that not all instances of poverty are immediately caused by sin, recognizes that "poverty and suffering are not inherently good. They are tragic distortions of God's good creation."[23] In this sense, poverty is much like sickness or disease. God in His sovereignty allows men and women to suffer from physical ailments, yet it is never His pleasure or delight that they do so. In the same way, though it is "God's will" that some remain poor, and even if He comforts them through the trial and uses the experience as a vehicle for their growth, it is never "God's wish" that they lack what they need.[24] The poverty that remains among God's people is a sign not that the kingdom is "now," but that it is still "not yet."

For this reason, we call upon pastors and leaders in The Christian and Missionary Alliance to challenge the poor in their congregations away from the false belief that God wishes for them to remain in their poverty. It is said that the Hebrew word for "be prosperous" (*tsalach*) means "to push forward; to break out mightily."[25] If this is so, it serves as an apt word picture for what God desires for them as part of the advancement of His kingdom. Poverty carries with it the idea of being bound up and contained. Prosperity would then be the poor person "breaking free" from that which keeps him or her confined, kept from enjoying the good gifts that God wishes to bestow.

But from a kingdom vantage point, how does a person "break free" and experience the blessing of God? Here we must refrain from the health-and-wealth gospel's tendency to trumpet "success formulas" and "rules of prosperity" that all but guarantee affluence to the faithful. Yet, as wrongheaded as the prosperity movement is, its error lies merely in the *distortion* of principles that are biblically true. In Jesus' parables, which stewards are the ones who receive the master's blessing? The ones who were faithful with the talents they were given!

We mentioned earlier that the rewards (Luke 12:44; 19:17, 19; Matthew 25:21-23) and punishments (Luke 12:46; 19:24; Matthew 25:30) in the parables are primarily eschatological, but that in the "realized eschatology" of the kingdom, they may be experienced in token form now. Without drawing dogmatic conclusions, we should be open to the possibility that material prosperity and poverty can be the result of our faithfulness and unfaithfulness in the use of God's wealth. Of course, we recognize that there are a variety of poverty situations in the church today and that their immediate causes are complex, which serves to warn against simple solutions. And we recognize that biblical teaching we have offered resembles the teaching in the Book of Proverbs: more general principle than specific promise (see, e.g., Proverbs 3:9-10). Nevertheless, the Bible appears to connect faithful stewardship with material blessing.

Two additional Old Testament passages bear out this link. First, Haggai testifies that the returning exiles, after becoming preoccupied with their own homes and forsaking the rebuilding of the Temple, suffered terrible poverty at the hand of God: "You have planted much, but harvested little. . . .You earn wages, only to put them in a purse with holes in it" (Haggai 1:6). But Haggai also testifies that when they reordered their priorities and began to spend their lives on God (1:12), the curse that had been on their crops, their livestock and their finances was lifted. The "holes in their purses" were closed. The crops in their fields began to yield good fruit. The material blessings of their God began to flow.[26] Second, Malachi proclaimed that the people of Israel during the Persian period were under the curse of God for robbing Him of His tithes and offerings (Malachi 3:9). But Malachi then offers to the people this promise from God: "Bring the whole tithe into the storehouse, that there may be food in my house. Test me in this . . . and see if I will not throw open the floodgates of heaven and pour out so much blessing that you will not have room enough for it" (3:10). Once again, the connection between faithful stewardship and material blessing is clear.

Our contention is that if the church embraces the reign and rule of God in the management of all its possessions, then it will see, as a by-product of the advancement of the kingdom, a powerful liberation of God's people. Christians will be released from their bondage under the spirit of Mammon, which keeps them impoverished, and be lifted to the joys of God's material blessing. If or when this happens, the Church must remember Luke 12:48: "From everyone who has been given much, much will be demanded; and from the one who has been entrusted with much, much more will be asked." It must be ready to preach the importance of generosity, hospitality, tithing and caring for the poor. Christians must strike a balance between the enjoyment of, and detachment from, their possessions. It is said that John Wesley often earned more than 1,400 pounds a year through the sale of his books, yet he normally spent less than thirty pounds on himself annually. The surplus he generously gave away. He wrote, "If I leave behind me ten pounds [when I die], you and all mankind bear witness against me that I lived and died a thief and a robber."[27] Wesley's self-abasement may seem radical and extreme, but it stands as a fine example of a kingdom mentality over one's wealth. Richard Foster wisely says, "We need instruction on how to possess money without being possessed by money. We need to learn how to own things without treasuring them. We need the disciplines that will allow us to live simply while managing great wealth and power."[28] This is the goal for our role as stewards in the kingdom of God that Jesus came to inaugurate.

C. The Spirit of the Tithe

Christians today disagree over the place of the tithe in the theology of stewardship. The intricacy of the debate is well illustrated by the interpretation of Abram's giving a tenth of his military spoils to Melchizedek, the first instance of the tithe in Scripture (Genesis 14:20).

Historically, the tenth, or a tithe, has always been symbolic of the whole. Immediately after the Genesis 14 event, Abram aligned his heart to God, the creator and possessor of all things (14:22). The tithe was a token symbol affirming that the whole belonged to God. Viewed this way, the amount or percentage given is not the issue with God. Rather, it is the spirit or the heart behind the gift. This, of course, does not mean the specifics of amount or percentage are unimportant. Perhaps it is best to affirm that both the heart and the specifics must come together as a single point of concern in the life of the disciple.

The spirit behind the tithe or "the spirit of the tithe" is seen and emphasized throughout the history of God's people.[29] We have already mentioned how Abram gave with no strings attached from a heart aligned to God (14:22). But sadly we see this heart diminish with Jacob, who, in Genesis 28:20-22, offers the second instance of a tithe. Jacob, the so-called "heel-grabber," tries to strike a bargain with God:

> Then Jacob made a vow, saying, "If God will be with me and will watch over me on this journey I am taking and will give me food to eat and clothes to wear so that I return safely to my father's house, then the LORD will be my God and this stone that I have set up as a pillar will be God's house, and of all that you give me I will give you a tenth."

In essence he is saying, "OK, God, here's the deal: If You do all these things for me, THEN, You will be my God and I will give You ten percent!" The spirit of the tithe that was behind his father's gift begins to wane in his own distorted covenant.

We mentioned earlier the various tithes in the Mosaic Law (Numbers 18:21-24; Deuteronomy 12:6-7; 14:22-29), but again, God's desire was for their hearts to be aligned to His heart first. Deuteronomy 14:23 says the purpose of the tithe was "so that you may learn to revere the LORD your God always." They were to give God the first and best of what they earned as an ongoing reminder that all they had belonged to Him. The law was never to be "performed" as a perfunctory obligation. It was intended to be an expression of a grace-birthed heart relationship with God. The spirit of the law was always more important to God than the letter of the law and correspondingly, the spirit of the tithe was always more important to God than the letter of the tithe.

The spirit of the tithe among the Pharisees of Jesus' day had all but disappeared (Matthew 6:2-4). In one passage, Jesus affirms the tithe, but rebukes the Pharisees for losing the spirit behind it: "You give a tenth of your spices—mint, dill and cummin. But you have neglected the more important matters of the law—justice, mercy and faithfulness. You should have practiced the latter, without neglecting the former" (23:23). Once again, the heart of the matter is the matter of the heart (c.f. 6:21).

Of course, there is a danger to this teaching on the spirit of the tithe. Some may say in response, "My heart is right with God—I don't have to give." Our reply is that this is a deceived position that is not built upon the testimony of Scripture. It comes from the spirit of Mammon and not the Spirit of God. The one harboring this mind-set is like the person who sins against his brother and then says, "I've confessed my sin in my heart before God. I don't have to make the situation right." The Spirit of God seeks not the "saying" alone, but also the "doing." In the words of James, "Faith without works is useless" (James 2:20, NASB). On the other hand, we must be just as quick to affirm the converse. Just as claiming the right heart without giving is wrong, so also giving without the right heart is equally wrong. The parable of Pharisee and the tax collector (Luke 18:9-14) reminds us that tithing is not to be regarded as a spiritual cure-all. What justified the non-tithing tax collector and condemned the tithing Pharisee was the state of their hearts.

On the subject of giving, the New Testament appears to de-emphasize the notion of percentage or amount. Nowhere does any New Testament writer call for a ten percent tithe.[30] If in fact the heart is the key issue and if we are merely stewards of what is ultimately owned by God, then the driving question we must put to ourselves is not, "How much do I give?" but "How much dare I keep?" The New Testament Church is to be filled with missionary people, not maintainers of the status quo! What a wonderful truth for The Christian and Missionary Alliance to proclaim as we move into this new millennium. The question must not be, "What percentage must I give?" but "How much dare I spend on myself?"

Perhaps here it would be helpful to suggest five practical, biblical principles to apply in this area of the spirit of the tithe. We should be encouraged to *give first*. Jesus says, "Give, and it will be given to you. A good measure, pressed down, shaken together and running over, will be poured into your lap. For with the measure you use, it will be measured to you" (Luke 6:38). The major purpose of the tithe was to remind the people that God comes first in our lives, that He alone deserves preeminence. The spirit of the tithe is well expressed in Proverbs 3:9-10: "Honor the LORD with your wealth, with the firstfruits of all your crops; then your barns will be filled to overflowing, and your vats will brim over with new wine."

An Alliance missionary tells the story of a young African boy who came to his door one day with a large fish in his hands. "Missionary, you taught us what tithing is, so here. I've brought you my tithe." As the missionary gratefully took the fish, he asked the boy, "If this is your tithe, where are the other nine fish?" At this, the boy smiled and said, "Back in the river. I'm going back to catch them now." To *give first* is a matter of faith and priority. It's not because we are spiritual that our tithe check is the first one we should write every week. It is because we are weak and forgetful, and we need that reminder of priority and heart alignment in our lives.

The second principle Scripture suggests is to *give cheerfully*. Paul says, "Remember this: Whoever sows sparingly will also reap sparingly, and whoever sows generously will also reap generously. Each man should give what he has decided in his heart to give, not reluctantly or under compulsion, for God loves a cheerful giver" (2 Corinthians 9:6-7).

We are reminded of this every year during tax season. During the year we rejoice at the paychecks and any extra income that comes in, but sometimes we flinch when we write our tithe and offering checks. When figuring our taxes we wince at every source of income and rejoice with every tithe and offering check—more income means more tax, but every tithe dollar means less tax. Everything is turned upside down or perhaps more appropriately, right side up. That is the perspective of eternity and the (hilarious?) spirit we need to have in our giving all year long!

The third principle is that we should *give faithfully*. When the master says, "Well done, good and faithful servant!" (Matthew 25:21-23) to the good stewards, he is speaking of reliability. Faithfulness is the heart of biblical stewardship. Faithfulness is in short supply in the church today. The church-growth experts are telling us that the new generations will not give the way the preceding generations gave. They are calling for new techniques and marketing strategies. While there are good aspects to these methods, they must never become a crutch to make up for our lack of faithfulness in stewardship. Adequate discipleship must call each new generation to be faithful sacrificially for the cause of the kingdom.

The fourth principle is that we should *give wisely*. Where we give our tithe and our offerings is an investment! Christians should give with wisdom. The church has lived through multiple financial scandals in recent years. Many failed churches and Christian organizations have been unwise in their stewardship. Hopefully, we can learn from others' mistakes. Thankfully, year after year The Christian and Missionary Alliance has been above reproach in our financial integrity. We can invite people to invest in the kingdom through the C&MA without reservation.

It is wise, we believe, to give first to one's home church. In First Corinthians 9:11, Paul says, "If we have sown spiritual seed among you, is it too much if we reap a material harvest from you?" The spiritual principle is simple: Give where you are being fed spiritually. Give where you see kingdom investments multiplying. Let us loudly and joyfully proclaim what God is doing through the ministry of The Christian and Missionary Alliance. Let us then assure our people that they are giving wisely when they entrust their finances to our care.

Finally, let us encourage our people to *give without seeking recognition*. Jesus saw the hypocrisy of the Pharisees' public giving and said, "But when you give to the needy [not if], do not let your left hand know what your right hand is doing, so that your giving may be in secret. Then your Father, who sees what is done in secret, will reward you" (Matthew 6:3-4). Secret giving is instructed not only because it guards against religious pride, but also because it is one of the primary ways God builds faith into our lives. If our confidence is in God, we will give without anyone else knowing and be content. Someone has rightly said, "Tithing is not God's method of raising money; it is His method of raising children." Giving without seeking recognition is an important part of that process.

Some years ago there was an Alliance church where the missionary pledges had regularly been collected and totaled during the last Sunday night service of the missionary conference. A very wealthy man in this congregation made it a practice to wait until the entire church had pledged, after which he would ceremoniously walk to the front with his pledge to increase the total dramatically. A new pastor had arrived at the church that year and he had been informed of the annual tradition. With great courage, he went to the large donor and explained the biblical concept of giving in secret. He informed him gently that it was inappropriate for his pledge to be public knowledge and that according to Scripture he was missing a greater blessing. The wealthy man graciously received the correction. The missionary pledge was higher than ever that year, and everyone involved received the reward of secret giving.

In a message on "Storehouse Tithing" the late Rev. Richard Harvey waited till the end of his message to take the offering. He said that if he were preaching on salvation he would have given the altar call at the end of the sermon so people could respond in obedience. Since the message was on giving, he wanted to take the offering at the end of the sermon to give us the opportunity to be obedient to the Lord in giving. After the offering he looked into the buckets, shaking his head, after the ushers had come back to the front. "Is that all you're willing to give for Jesus? Send them around again!" Although that utterance sounds abusive, apparently that moment was actually one of great joy and excitement.

"I remember digging deeper into my own pockets and putting in the money my mother had given me for ice cream that night," Rev. Ron Walborn said. "I felt for perhaps the first time (but thankfully not the last) the wonderful privilege of sacrificial, yet joyful giving. I do not remember the details of that message, but I will never forget Rev. Harvey's passion and the text of Scripture from which he preached. Both have influenced and shaped my view of stewardship to this day."

" 'Bring the whole tithe into the storehouse, that there may be food in my house. Test me in this,' says the LORD Almighty, 'and see if I will not throw open the floodgates of heaven and pour out so much blessing that you will not have room enough for it' " (Malachi 3:10).

D. The Stranglehold of Debt

The final issue related to biblical stewardship is the stranglehold of debt. Many believers in this nation are unable to obey the clear directives of God because they cannot pay off money owed and its accruing interest. They are in bondage to the tyrannical demands of debt. The story is told of two men talking about money. One asked the other, "Joe, what would you do if you had all the money in the world?" Joe thought for a moment and replied, "I'd apply it to my debts as far as it would go!" We may laugh at Joe's reply, but many of us have felt the same way about the size of our accumulating debts. And far too many Christians are in deep despair because they foolishly underestimated their ability to pay them back.

Incurring large amounts of debt has become a lifestyle in our nation. This year, the federal government will spend more money on interest than was spent on the entire federal budget in 1962. *The Wall Street Journal* recently reported that fifty-one percent of all corporate profits are now being eaten up by interest on debt. The average American family holds a credit card debt of $7,000 on seven to eight credit cards. This is in addition to their debt on cars and RVs.[31] A recent Gallup poll showed that fifty-six percent of people having undergone divorce cited "financial tensions in the home related to debt" as a significant factor.[32]

Our stewardship teaching must address this problem or it will fail to produce effective disciples. Several years ago an Alliance pastor felt the Lord directing him to preach a series of sermons on what the Scripture says about debt. First, he searched the Word of God. Then, he thought about his own financial situation. Suddenly he realized he was in no position to preach on the issue. Beyond that, he had been sinning in the area of financial stewardship and was in need of repentance and restitution. At that point, he and his wife began a serious attempt to pay off all of their debts as quickly as possible and live according to biblical principles of stewardship, rather than the culture's "consumer discipleship." Three years later, they were completely debt-free and were able to say, "Yes," when God called them to take a ministry position that paid considerably less than their previous salary. Debt reduction had freed them to be obedient to God's call.

Two stories in the Old Testament illustrate the ways in which wise people operate toward debt. First, in Genesis 14, after Abram returns captured goods to the King of Sodom and is offered the chance to keep them for himself (14:21), he refuses with these words: "I have raised my hand to the LORD, God Most High, Creator of heaven and earth, and have taken an oath that I will accept nothing belonging to you, not even a thread or the thong of a sandal, so that you will never be able to say, 'I made Abram rich.' " (14:22-23). Although the goods were apparently a free gift from the king of Sodom, Abram shrewdly saw that there were unspoken strings attached. Receiving them would result in an ungodly obligation to an evil king. He wisely refused to take on the debt.

Second, in Second Kings 4:1-7, the widow who was about to lose her sons as slaves to a creditor exhibits good sense in the way she gets out of debt. (a) She cries out for help to the man of God (4:1). In other words, she sought God and wise counsel as her first step in her dilemma with debt. (b) She assumes, with Elisha's prompting, that she must pay her debts (4:2). She did not act as the wicked, who "borrow and do not repay" (Psalm 37:21). (c) She was willing to part with what she had (2 Kings 4:2). The little oil she offered to the prophet started her on the road to financial freedom. Such detachment from our nonnegotiable possessions is possible when we believe that all truly belongs to God. (d) She trusted God to multiply her efforts (4:3-7). By listening to the man of God, little became much.

The Book of Proverbs does not forbid the borrowing of money or goods, but it does point out the dangers associated with taking on debt. Proverbs 24:27 says, "Finish your outdoor work and get your fields ready; after that, build your house." The wise man admonishes us to work hard at ensuring a source of income *before* improving our comfort.

He may also be warning against "purchasing large numbers of goods before we have earned the money to pay for them."[33] Proverbs also warns against being a cosigner for someone else's debts: "A man lacking in judgment strikes hands in pledge and puts up security for his neighbor" (17:18). The reason, of course, is that the cosigner is in danger of losing his possessions, including his very own bed, if the borrower defaults (22:26-27).

Finally, the Mosaic law offers a few insights into the dangers of debt. The blessings and curses at Mt. Gerizim and Mt. Ebal in Deuteronomy 28 mention debt. To be blessed is to "lend to many nations" and to "borrow from none" (28:12) and to be cursed is to borrow from the alien and to lend to none (28:44). The law also limited what could be offered as collateral on loans to protect a debtor from terrible harm if he failed to pay. When Deuteronomy 24:6 forbids a pair of millstones from being put up as security, it is protecting the debtor's livelihood, so that, in the event of default, he will not be condemned to perpetual indebtedness. When Deuteronomy 24:12-13 requires a creditor who has taken the debtor's cloak as collateral to return it at night, God is protecting a person's ability to keep warm, a basic necessity of life. The same law also protects the debtor's dignity. The creditor could not go into the debtor's house to take the security; he could only stand outside and wait for the debtor to bring it out to him (24:10-11). In these ways, the Mosaic law recognizes the destructiveness and humiliation uncontrolled debt can bring upon a person.

To summarize: The Old Testament 1) warns against borrowing money and goods we are not prepared to pay back; 2) recognizes the threat uncontrolled debt can be to our well-being. The New Testament continues the Old Testament's warning about debt. Romans 13:8 says, "Let no debt remain outstanding, except the continuing debt to love one another . . ." although a more literal translation presents a more strict prohibition: "Owe nothing to anyone (Greek: *medeni meden opheilete*) except to love one another . . ." (NASB). It is debatable whether this verse denies all loans, including student loans and home mortgages. The goal in applying it is not to be legalistic or to foist false guilt but to ask ourselves, "Are my finances headed in the direction Scripture is pointing? By God's grace, am I heading for freedom in this area of my life?"

We will never get free from the grip of Mammon or debt until we learn and practice the spiritual disciplines of contentment and simplicity. In his groundbreaking book, *Margin*, Dr. Richard Swenson dissects the pathology of our debt-ridden culture: "Discontent as a driving force for a society might make that society rich, but it will bankrupt it in the end."[34] Swenson correctly points out that God not only *commends* contentment (1 Timothy 6:6), He *commands* it: ". . . be content with what you have" (Hebrews 13:5). Unfortunately, in our debt-driven culture, "our quest is usually not for contentment but for more."[35] The full context of First Timothy 6 is worth noting here:

> But godliness with contentment is great gain. For we brought nothing into the world, and we can take nothing out of it. But if we have food and clothing, we will be content with that. People who want to get rich fall into temptation and a trap and into many foolish and harmful desires that plunge men into ruin and destruction. For the love of money is a root of all kinds of evil. Some people, eager for money, have wandered from the faith and pierced themselves with many griefs. (6:6-10)

At the root of much (not all) of our debt is greed and the spirit of verses 9 and 10. If this is true, then we must repent and find forgiveness. It is time to align our hearts with God and our financial priorities with His Word.

It is not the will of God for His people to be enslaved by debt. Indeed, the whole message of the gospel is about Jesus paying a debt we could not pay. His heart's desire is that His people be free in all areas of their lives.

> And when you were dead in your transgressions and the uncircumcision of your flesh, He made you alive together with Him, having forgiven us all our transgressions, having canceled out the certificate of debt consisting of decrees against us *and* which was hostile to us; and He has taken it out of the way, having nailed it to the cross. (Colossians 2:13-14, NASB, emphasis added)

One final point in relation to this issue of debt impacts our mission in The Christian and Missionary Alliance. How do we reconcile the massive amount of debt being taken on by our young people in their college and seminary training with the biblical teaching in this area? During premarital counseling, a young couple who was graduating from one of our Alliance colleges revealed over $40,000 in debt between them. This couple is now in ministry in the Alliance. They would like to go on to seminary, but the debt load from college makes it impossible for them to continue. Many would say that an education is an appreciating expense, and therefore is allowable under biblical standards for debt. This is an issue that needs much thought and prayer. Could it be that we have been discipled more in the ways of our culture on the issue of debt, than we have in the ways of the kingdom?

Summary

For a multitude of reasons, The Christian and Missionary Alliance must rekindle its passion to become godly stewards—men and women who handle God's resources with integrity. Our vision to become "a movement of Great Commission Christians who are glorifying God by building Christ's Church worldwide," will only be realized if we make a wholesale commitment of all we have and all we are to Him. Stewardship is the foundational piece of the larger context of Christian discipleship. The Scripture calls us to be wise and faithful stewards who are responsible and accountable for handling life, money, spiritual gifts and the gospel message according to God's purposes. As Richard Niebuhr says, "Stewardship is everything we do after we accept Christ." Through the power of the Holy Spirit, let us seek to be and to train up godly stewards. May God give us the courage to see these stewardship issues through kingdom lenses. May we be willing to go against the grain of our culture in order to raise up the next generation of disciples for Jesus Christ.

Endnotes

1. Dallas Willard, *The Divine Conspiracy* (San Francisco: HarperCollins, 1998), 15.

2. Walter Bauer, *Greek English Lexicon of the New Testament and Early Christian Literature, 2nd ed.* (Chicago: University Press, 1979), 511.

3. This is most notably the position of classic dispensationalism, which has interpreted Jesus' kingdom language as a future "millennial" kingdom.

4. C.H. Dodd, *The Parables of the Kingdom* (New York: Charles Scribner's Sons, 1958), 44.

5. G.E. Ladd, *The Gospel of the Kingdom* (Grand Rapids: Eerdmans, 1959).

6. A.B. Simpson, *The Grace of Giving*, C&MA National Office.

7. We will not address in this paper the question of the stewardship responsibility of all mankind for the care of the earth and natural resources. Our colleague at Nyack College, Dr. Elio Cuccaro, addresses the question, "Does all mankind have a stewardship from God?" in his editorial, "The Stewardship of Mankind," in the 1999 *Alliance Academic Review*, pp. ix-xii. Our focus will be on the stewardship responsibility of believers.

8. There are several full-scale studies on stewardship that are fruitful for study and meditation. Among the few that we would recommend are Ronald J. Sider, *Rich Christians in an Age of Hunger*, 20th Anniversary Revision (Nashville: Word Publishing, 1997) and Craig L. Blomberg, *Neither Poverty Nor Riches* (Grand Rapids: Eerdmans, 1999).

9. *Merriam-Webster's Collegiate Dictionary*, 10th ed. (Springfield, MA: Merriam-Webster, 1996), 1154.

10. Walter Elwell, *The Evangelical Dictionary of Theology* (Grand Rapids: Baker, 1984), 1054.

11. James D. Berkley, *Leadership Handbook of Management and Administration* (Grand Rapids: Baker, 1997), 407. The charity tithe took place every three years. We should also note other payments the people of Israel were required to make. A civil tithe imposed by future kings is predicted by Samuel in First Samuel 8:15-17. Further, a sanctuary tax imposed upon every male twenty years or older is set at half a shekel per year in Exodus 30:11-16 and at a third of a shekel in Nehemiah 10:32-35.

12. The disciples illustrate this expectancy with their question in Acts 1:6: "Are you at this time going to restore the kingdom to Israel?"

13. The parallel in Matthew 24:45-51 also occurs immediately after a warning about the coming of the Son of Man (Matthew 24:44).

14. Bauer, *Greek-English Lexicon*, 560.

15. John MacArthur, *Commentary on Matthew 1-7* (Chicago: Moody, 1985), 415.

16. Richard Foster, *Money, Sex and Power* (San Francisco: HarperCollins, 1989), 26.

17. David Johnson, "The Spirit of the Tithe" (sermon tape, n.d.), Growing in Grace Media Ministries, Crystal, MN.

18. This story was told to me (Ron) at a YWAM training base in 1997. The man telling me was with a team led by John Dawson. I have seen this story confirmed several times in the writings of John Dawson and other YWAM missionaries.

19. Among the most prominent leaders in the movement are Kenneth Hagin, Kenneth and Gloria Copeland, Jerry Savelle and Fred Price. For a good analysis of the health-and-wealth gospel, see Dennis Hollinger, "Enjoying God Forever: An Historical/Sociological Profile of the Health and Wealth Gospel," *Trinity Journal*, n.s. 9 (1988), 131-149; Bruce Barron, *The Health and Wealth Gospel* (Downers Grove, IL: InterVarsity, 1987); D.R. McConnell, *A Different Gospel* (Peabody, MA: Hendrickson, 1988).

20. Kenneth Copeland, *The Laws of Prosperity* (Fort Worth, TX: Kenneth Copeland Publications, 1974); Kenneth Hagin, *How to Write Your Own Ticket with God* (Tulsa, OK: Faith Library, 1978).

21. Frederick Price, *Faith, Foolishness or Presumption?* (Tulsa: Harrison House, 1979).

22. E.W. Kenyon, *Jesus the Healer* (Seattle: Kenyon's Gospel Publishing Society, 1943); Kenneth Hagin, *Authority of the Believer* (Tulsa: Faith Library, 1967).

23. Sider, *Rich Christians in an Age of Hunger*, 113.

24. See Millard Erickson, *Christian Theology*, vol. 1 (Grand Rapids: Baker, 1983), 361, for the distinction between God's wish (e.g., His opposition to the sinful, murderous intentions of Jesus' executors) and God's will (e.g., His decree that Jesus should die on the cross). The first is more general and has to do with the values that please God. The second is more specific and has to do with what God sovereignly decides will actually occur.

25. *Strong's Greek and Hebrew Dictionary*, reference 6743.

26. Ron's unpublished dissertation from Fuller Seminary is entitled, *Breaking the Spirit of Poverty: Perspectives on Wealth and Poverty from the Prophet Haggai*. See this work for more information on this subject.

27. Quoted in Sider, *Rich Christians in an Age of Hunger*, 164.

28. Richard Foster, *Money, Sex and Power*, 46.

29. I (Ron) owe a great debt of gratitude to Rev. David Johnson for much of the material in this section. His tape series, "The Spirit of the Tithe," has helped to shape my own theology significantly in this area.

30. Paul in First Corinthians 16:2 says one should give in keeping with one's income, a reference perhaps to percentage, but no specification of ten percent.

31. *Crown Ministries Small Group Financial Manual* (Longwood, FL: Crown Ministries, 1995), 37. Crown Ministries has one of the best discipleship/stewardship programs available. I strongly recommend their ministry.

32. Howard Dayton, *Your Money Counts* (Longwood, FL: Crown Ministries, 1996), 34.

33. Wayne Grudem, *The Bible and Economic Decisions*, unpublished manuscript for my (Frank) seminary ethics class at Trinity Evangelical Divinity School.

34. Richard Swenson, *Margin* (Colorado Springs: NavPress, 1992), 186.

35. Ibid., 187.

Negative Jewish Reaction to Protestant Missions to the Jews from the 1880s to Recent Days: Will It Ever End?

Daniel J. Evearitt

The Christian and Missionary Alliance has always held that the Jewish people are spiritually lost without a personal saving relationship with Jesus Christ, their Messiah. This lostness of the Jew without Christ was emphasized by Alliance founder A.B. Simpson, who wrote, "The Jew will be judged by the law and the measure of light that he has received through the Old Testament, and he, too will be found condemned by the verdict of his own Scriptures and conscience."[1]

The place of the Jewish people in Bible prophecy was indicated by Simpson in his book *The Gospel of the Kingdom* (1890). While Israel had once been the "chief of the nations," he wrote, "now the kingdom passed from the chosen people to the Gentile nations, and hereafter we see Israel in subjection." Simpson asserted that the Jewish people faced severe hardships because of their rejection of Jesus as their Messiah. These harsh judgments included "the withdrawal of the gospel from them and the transfer of their privileges to the Gentiles," "the destruction of Jerusalem and the dispersion of the Jews among all the nations," and the "subsequent Jewish oppressions" down to the present day, all of which "was but the fulfillment of Divine warnings and judgments which had been repeated by almost every prophet from Moses to Malachi."[2]

All was not lost for the Jewish people, however. According to Simpson's reading of Bible prophecy, "all through the Christian age a remnant shall be saved," preserved as a people through the years and returned to their land. He projected that, as a nation, the Jewish people would eventually turn to redemption in Christ.[3]

Mission work among the Jewish people has been part of the worldwide missionary outreach of the Alliance since the 1890s.[4] Alliance members have been convinced that the nonbelieving world is spiritually lost outside of Christ's redemption, and that included in this number are nonbelieving Jews.

It seems there has always been tension between Christians and Jews when it comes to the matter of evangelization. From the first centuries of the church, through the height of Jewish immigration at the end of the nineteenth century and right up to today's Southern Baptist prayer guides and Messianic-Jewish outreach groups, spokespersons for the Jewish community have objected to the fact, theology and methods of missions to the Jews. By looking back through American religious history to the late nineteenth century, a pattern of reaction can be seen. Repeated objections are raised. Ominous worry is voiced. Charges are leveled.

In 1889 Isaac M. Wise published a blistering attack on Protestant missionary activity in the Jewish community. He declared in *A Defense of Judaism Versus Proselytizing Christianity*:

> If you read the pages of history, ancient and modern, the misery, sorrow, affliction, destruction of life and happiness which the conversion mania, the proselytizing fury did bring and brings now over millions of innocent men, women and children, simply because they cannot think with other people's brains and would not be seduced to hypocrisy before God and man, you will be forced to admit that the conversion mania and proselytizing fury is an outrage on religion, is a blasphemy on the Most High, a curse to the cause of humanity, hence the reverse, the direct opposite, of true religion.[5]

He continued, "From the pulpit, in journals, tracts and books, by learned and illiterate, the loyal and the renegade, the sincere and the hypocrite, the sane and the insane, we are incessantly assailed and attacked, wounded and mortified in the most tender spots of man's heart." All this, he said, was done in the slim hope that Jews would "retrograde from Judaism to Christianity, or that Christology ever could become the universal religion of the human family." The "unreasoning mania" had reached the "very doors of our temples," wrote Wise, and "perverts the heads of clergymen to establish and maintain missions to the Jews." He proclaimed, "It is time to defend our own, or else our silence might lead unsophisticated people to believe that we groan under the ban of ignorance, superstition and fanaticism, and the conversionists are the truly good people."[6]

Wise charged the proselytizers with disrupting "natural and beautiful family relations" and destroying ties between spouses, parents and children. This "work of proselyting Christianity" was criminal activity, he argued, done "without any compunction of conscience, simply because that mania is no longer under the control of conscience." The church may "save a soul" but in the process "conversionists every day of the year perpetuate any amount of wickedness besides the bribery which they apply . . . the serpentile seduction which they try, the hypocrisy which they cultivate," he concluded, so that "they save a soul by diabolic means."[7]

Christian conversionists were accused by Wise of turning the Bible upside down in an effort to prove that Jesus was the Messiah. He called their use of Scriptures a "pious fraud . . . intended only to beguile unsophisticated, credulous and devout people to accept the sham evidence upon their teacher's word and wit."[8]

Rabbi Solomon Schindler argued that "Jesus was not the founder of Christianity, that he never planned it nor laid its foundations." He asserted that Jesus' "personality has been brought into the Church, and used as its cornerstone." Furthermore, he claimed, "there are no historical sources from which we could derive authentic information concerning his life, his deeds, and his death."[9]

Schindler's defense of Judaism is an attack upon the claims of Christianity. St. Paul created Christianity, according to Schindler. "Paul was no rabbi," he charged. "He was no scholar whatsoever." Schindler said of Paul:

> Observing that Judaism could not and would not allow one letter of the law to be changed, he embraced with eagerness the legends of the crucified Jesus, which must have reached him in an exaggerated form;

and without having ever known him, he made him the cornerstone of the building which he proposed to erect. There was an old saying, that the Messiah would do away with the law. . . . Paul made use of it, and accepted Jesus as the Messiah, no matter whether he had fulfilled what was expected of a Messiah or not. . . . [H]e admitted Gentiles into Judaism without the performance of the Abrahamic rite, and allowed them to eat whatever they pleased.[10]

At Paul's hand, Schindler claimed, the Jewish messiah idea became the universal Son of God.

The Protestant missionary outreach in Jewish neighborhoods was of deep concern to the religious leaders of the Jewish community. They were especially concerned that Christianizers were attempting to lure Jewish children into converting to Christianity. A.M. Radin, chaplain to the Jewish Minister's Association of New York, reported in *The American Hebrew* that when he began his work in prisons and asylums he was informed that "hundreds of Jewish children are being entangled in the nets of Christian Missionary Schools." Upon investigation he discovered that "the pious teachers distribute among the small Jewish pupils candies and dolls; to the bigger ones shoes, dresses, hats, etc., to induce them to attend the school regularly." He discovered, as well, that the pupils were "instructed not to tell their parents that they have to sing Christian hymns there or that they are taught the dogmas and doctrines of Christianity.

"Some of the parents," he noted, being recent immigrants from Russia and Romania, "had no idea" that the school was a "Christian institution with proselytizing tendencies." Consequently, Radin reported, "I visited nearly all the Jewish families on Eldridge, Delancy and Stanton streets and informed the parents of the pernicious anti-Jewish tendencies to which their children were exposed in this school." While some of them ordered their children to stop attending the school, others resented his interference. "Of about 200 Jewish pupils attending the Christian Missionary Schools," he admitted, "I could influence only 47 to leave them, so far."[11]

An editorial in *The American Hebrew* in 1895 pointed out that Russian immigrants in the Bronx were being infiltrated by Christian missionaries. Russian immigrant children "have been attracted to the Christian

Sunday School," it noted, "induced by religious playmates or by the temptation of gifts and treats that are held out by those in charge of these schools, who find nothing wrong in so doing."[12]

The charge of bribery was often laid at the door of Protestant missions to the Jews by Jewish leaders because of the practice of giving treats and gifts to children who attended mission schools. While the missionaries may have thought this to be a perfectly innocent gesture of warmth and love toward the children, it was most always interpreted by the Jewish critics of missionary efforts as an attempt to lure Jewish children away from their religion by coercive methods.

The American Hebrew published an editorial entitled "Are We Asleep, or Do We Merely Shut Our Eyes?" in 1893, designed to direct the attention of the Jewish community to the dangers of missionary activity in the Jewish community, especially trade schools designed to train young Jews to sew and, at the same time, to dispense Christianity. It pointed to Christian missionary schools that were "prosecuting a most active work in Christianizing Jews" and asked, "If Christian congregations combine to do the much needed missionary work, and missionary work is only the effort to reclaim from crime and wretchedness, to regenerate lives that are suffering from the destroying forces that flourish in irremediable poverty, why cannot our Jewish congregations combine to do the same?" The editorial noted that the reaction to proselytizing trade schools in the poorer Jewish neighborhoods so far had been indifference. In fact, it said that influential Jewish leaders had laughed when told that Christians were setting up schools, and that the leaders made "no effort to discover its magnitude, or if the Jews in that quarter require any saving hand, and when in time they hear of a Jewish proselyte, they spurn him and denounce the proselytizer."[13]

When *The American Hebrew* brought missionary schools for children to the attention of the Jewish community a couple of years before, "a great hue and cry was raised" against the missionary. The missionary defended his actions by stating that "he opened this school because the children he solicited were totally neglected, left completely to the influences of their degraded surroundings." The editorial admitted that there was no Jewish effort to help these children and that, rather than blame the missionary, Jews should get active in aiding their own people so that Christians would not have to. Once again Jews were asked to fill a social welfare need by supplying vocational training, so that Christian proselytizers would not be able to use free trade schools as a platform to preach Christianity in the Jewish neighborhoods.[14]

The issue of Christians stepping in to do what Jews should do for themselves was also presented by Minnie D. Louis at the Jewish Women's Congress in Chicago in 1893. She addressed the topic, "Mission Work Among the Unenlightened Jews," telling the women that "when we see today Christian Missions springing up among our neglected Jews, we have no right to condemn them; it is we who deserve the condemnation for unfaithfulness to our duty."[15]

Learning that "missionaries are making most active efforts at converting the children of recently arrived immigrants in Boston," an 1895 editorial in *The American Hebrew* urged, "The Jews of Boston should unite in establishing schools which will counteract these efforts."[16] Later that year, *The American Hebrew* issued another call for more Jewish education, noting the increased "efforts of missionaries to Christianize children of Jewish parents, not only among the poor, but even among the well-to-do."[17]

By the end of the nineteenth century numerous efforts to educate Jewish children were underway in New York and other cities under the auspices of the Educational Alliance and other Jewish organizations. Much of this was in direct response to Christian missionary activity in the poorer Jewish neighborhoods. The earlier German-Jewish immigrants, much to their credit, responded to the need to educate Jewish children and to offer classes in English language study for adults. Beside the impetus of combating conversionist schools, the German Jews also saw a need to Americanize their Jewish brethren from Eastern Europe. A vast effort was made to aid the incoming immigrants in adapting to American life.

Not only did *The American Hebrew* chastise Jewish leaders for not providing educational opportunities for poor Jewish children, it also noted the religious vacuum many Jews were experiencing in America. The editorial "Work to be Done" warned, "We have been so busy Americanizing the foreign contingent that the religious needs of those who have been reared among us have been utterly overlooked. The result has been that many have been brought under Christian influences, or, what is still worse, have sunk into religious indifference from which they cannot be roused." It had come to the attention of the editors that some Jewish women "have allowed their children to attend Christian Sunday-schools rather than bring them up with no religious influence, and that they themselves became attached to Christian movements in order to satisfy longings within them."[18]

The charge that Jewish religion did not meet the spiritual needs of the Jewish people was made repeatedly by Christian evangelists. Jews were seen as being spiritually adrift in America and, therefore, fair game for Christian conversionist activities. The countercharge made by Jewish leaders was that Judaism satisfied the needs of its adherents and that only spiritual misfits within the Jewish community were attracted to Christianity.

The American Hebrew responded to an article in *The Churchman* which, after expounding on the contributions of Jews to the life and thought of the modern world, concluded by stating, "What we do desire is that the descendants of Abraham should become followers of Christ." *The American Hebrew* asked, "Why? Would it make us more honest, more humane, more charitable, more patriotic?" It declared that conversion activity was counterproductive.[19]

Rabbi Louis Weiss was moved by the accusation of "some missionaries and some fanatics" that Jews are "blind and stubborn for not believing in Christ," to write *Some Burning Questions: An Exegetical Treatise on the Christianizing of Judaism* (1893). Although he was reluctant to be critical of the beliefs of others, he felt compelled to defend Judaism from Christian attackers.[20] Weiss condemned the message of some Christian ministers: "Any faith that menaces the peace of and creates prejudice against another faith . . . is an impure faith, void of the essence that would signalize it as God's truth."[21]

Weiss was vexed by the question, "Did Christianity supersede Judaism?" He answered, "While Christianity was conceived in and born from the womb of Israel's creed, and has become the predominant religion, it does not follow that Judaism became extinct." He based his answer on the fact that the New Testament does not say Judaism was obsolete, nor did Jesus say anything that indicated that that was so. In fact, noted Weiss, "Jesus was a Jew and had never renounced his religion, nor did he teach aught contrary to the law of Moses and the precepts of the prophets."[22]

All men who follow the true religion, which for Weiss consisted of "to collect, to bind fast, to cement the human family into fraternal relationship," were "acceptable" before God. It was his belief that people should stay in the religion into which they were born. "The one born from a Christian mother, raised, trained and educated by Christian parents, will grow up a Christian," he wrote, "while one born of a Jewish mother, raised, trained and educated by Jewish parents, will grow up a Jew. This is the rule; the exception is exceedingly rare." Weiss added, "For each teaches to love God and our fellowman, and the one who hates his neighbor because he professes a different religion, is neither Jew nor Christian; he is a bigot, a fanatic."[23]

Rabbi B. Felsenthal addressed a mixed audience of Christians and Jews in Chicago in 1893 on the topic, "Why Do Jews Not Accept Jesus as Their Messiah?" Three years earlier Felsenthal had been dismayed that a conference for Christians and Jews at a local Chicago church turned out to have been organized and operated by a missionary to the Jews. Unfortunately the true purpose of the conference was not discovered until after it was underway and some rabbis had been persuaded to take part in it. He deplored the deception of such a device. He now wanted to go on record as being firmly opposed to missions to the Jews.[24]

Felsenthal urged those who pressed the question of why Jews do not accept Jesus as their Messiah to go to the Unitarians, the Free Religion Association or Ethical Culture and ask them why they do not accept Jesus as the Messiah. Or, they should go to the nominal Christians or the average man and ask them why they do not believe in the Messiah, Jesus. They would find, he was sure, that belief in Jesus as the Messiah was as firmly held in the average person's mind as it was in the minds of "Thomas Jefferson, Charles Sumner, William Ellery Channing, Theodore Parker, or Ralph Waldo Emerson." He told his Christian listeners,

> you have a large field for your endeavors to convert and 'save' your infidel gentile brethren, and you ought indeed first try to reconquer these unbelieving sons and daughters of Christian parents and to bring them back to the Christian fold, before you proceed with your missionary work among these obstinate and benighted Jews . . . as you are used to call them.

Furthermore, Felsenthal told them "you ought to try and convert your own backsliders first. . . . [G]o to the tens of thousands of unchurched ones. . . . And after you have succeed in 'saving' them, then dear friends, will it be time enough to 'save' us stiffnecked and obstinate Jews."[25]

When it comes to "so-called" Messianic passages in the Old Testament, Felsenthal accused the Christian conversionists of taking verses out of context and reading their own thoughts into the Bible. He further charged that the New Testament wrongly interpreted the Old Testament. He said that no other book in the world had suffered so much from false interpretation as the Bible had.[26]

In the end Felsenthal urged that Christians and Jews agree to disagree and put their energies into working for peace and harmony in the world.[27]

Upset by letters to the Jewish press from Protestant clergymen in an effort to convince Jews that Jesus was their Messiah, Lewis Hart wrote *A Jewish Reply to Christian Evangelists* (1906). "When Christian ministers take to writing to Jewish newspapers for the purpose of furthering their proselytizing schemes," he declared, "it is time to repel their attacks."[28]

Despite the fact that Christians had for nineteen centuries "afflicted" Jews with supposed "proofs," Hart asserted, "they have always failed to influence Jewish beliefs, because, among other reasons, they have always adopted a line of argument that has only evoked Jewish contempt."[29]

Rejecting the Christian doctrine of the Trinity on the grounds that it is not supported by Scripture, Hart attacked the idea that Jews should worship a new god, the one presented to them by Christians as the "Lord Jesus Christ." If God had wanted the Jewish people to worship Jesus as their God, claimed Hart, "He would have said so in language as plain and unmistakable as that of any of the Ten Commandments, in words so plain that there could be no debate and no possibility of mistake about them."[30]

Judaism, argued Hart, is not an exclusive religion. The allowance has always been made by Judaism that the "pious and virtuous of all faiths have an equal share in the happiness of the future life." While Jews respect the right of Christians to worship God in their manner, he asked that Christians respect Jews and let them worship in their own manner.[31]

Lamenting the fact that Jews were besieged by "conversionist attacks," not by logic, facts or appeals but by "temptations of material aid and comforts and benefits," Nathan Joseph penned *Why I Am Not a Christian: A Reply to the Conversionists* in 1908. He presented arguments against the doctrines of the Trinity, vicarious atonement, original sin, eternal punishment and mediation. Christianity, at its inception, wrote Joseph, was "Judaism freed from the heavy yoke of priestly forms and ordinances," a premature effort to realize "the messianic vision of peace and goodwill among men and the dream of the Kingdom of God upon earth." The morality of Jesus, he claimed, was not Christianity; "it was the morality of Judaism, pure and simple."[32]

Louis Wirth sheds some light on the long history of Jewish conversion to Christianity when, in his book *The Ghetto* (1928), he describes the effect of conversion on the tightknit Jewish communities of Europe:

> Sometimes a Jew would leave the ghetto and, enticed by the opportunities that were supposed to await him outside, become a convert to Christianity; and sometimes these converts, broken and humiliated, would return to the ghetto to taste again of the warm, intimate, tribal life that was to be found nowhere but among their own people. On such occasion the romance of the renegade would be told in the ghetto streets, and the whole community would thereby be welded into a solid mass, clinging more tenaciously than ever to its old traditions.[33]

The Jewish community in Chicago in the 1920s retained some of the cohesiveness that protected the European ghettos from conversion to Christianity, according to Wirth. He maintained that Protestant missions to the Jews had been able to make "no appreciable progress in converting any Jews there." Although intermarriage was becoming much more common between Jews and Christians since the disintegration of the ghetto, Wirth found that there was "probably little conversion to the established Christian denominations."[34]

Trude Weiss-Rosmarin's 1943 book, *Judaism and Christianity*, recapitulates some of the differences that Jewish critics of missions to the Jews laid out above. It discusses the chief difference, that Judaism was "pure and uncompromising monotheism," as well as Judaism's rejection of the doctrines of original sin, vicarious atonement and mediation. *Judaism and Christianity* also disputes Christianity's rejection of Mosaic law and that Judaism has been superseded by Christianity. It traces the enmity between Christianity and Judaism back to the New Testament which "represents Judaism as a stunted, backward and obsolete religion without 'fulfilment' and lacking 'truth.'" The charge made by earlier critics of Christian theology is repeated here, that Christians distorted the text of the Old Testament to prove that Jesus Christ was the promised Messiah. It claims that "[t]he Church adopted the Hebrew Bible for no other reason than that it regarded it as a book of prophecies foretelling Jesus' career." And that "[e]ntire libraries have been written to prove 'Christian fulfilments' foreshadowed in the Hebrew Bible." The New Testament writers were forced, according to Weiss-Rosmarin, to make every trivial detail foretold about the Messiah fit Jesus Christ; as a result, the Hebrew Bible was interpreted in a way "diametrically opposed to the meaning with which tradition invested" it.[35]

The failure of Protestant missions to the Jews to make many converts among the Jews of New York in the early nineteenth century is asserted by Hyman B. Grinstein in *The Rise of the Jewish Community of New York 1654-1860*. Despite strenuous efforts by societies and individuals to "missionize the Jews . . . [i]n the majority of cases those efforts failed miserably." Those "few Jewish apostates in New York City were usually denounced as swindlers," noted Grinstein. Pamphlets were designed with a "fraudulant purpose in mind," he wrote. "Names like 'Joseph and Benjamin' or 'Judah's Lion' were designed to trap the unwary." Grinstein reported, "The citations in the periodical press on missionary work among the Jews and the replies to their efforts are numerous. *The Jewish Miscellany*, published by the American Jewish Publication Society, had as one of its purposes," according to him, "spreading the knowledge of Judaism among the Jews in order to combat intermarriage and apostasy."[36]

Grinstein reported that the very first Jewish periodical published in America, *The Jew*, was not so much a periodical as it was a "continuing polemic against Christian missionary activity."[37]

The accusation of deceptive measures was lodged against nineteenth-century mission groups by Grinstein. In New York City, the American Bible Society permitted a sign to be placed on their building which read, "Jews Society, Room 36." Any unsuspecting Jew going to that room would find the offices of the American Society for Meliorating the Condition of the Jews. The names of periodicals published by mission organizations, he claimed, were deliberately misleading, i.e., *The Jewish Chronicle* and *The Israelite Indeed*.[38]

"Apostasy was rare," according to Grinstein, and the apostate in America was always considered a "traitor" to Judaism and was "excluded" from the Jewish community.[39]

The belief that America is a "Protestant country" has lived on into the twentieth century. This is the opinion of Stuart E. Rosenberg, who wrote in 1964:

> To be sure, America in federal law was never a "Christian nation." But in the light of social realities the atmosphere of American life, not only in the Puritan communities, on the frontier, and in rural areas, but also in the early twentieth-century cities was Christian in everything but law.

Second-generation Jewish immigrants, according to Rosenberg, believed that in order to become "fully American" Jews should cast off their religious traditions. Unlike other ethnic immigrant groups, who blended into churches of their own home-country denominations, Jews who cast aside their ethnic identity also rejected their religious heritage. For with the "jettisoning of their Jewishness, their Judaism too was unloaded," and they became what Rosenberg called "inverted Maronnos," nonpracticing Jews who remained Jews.[40]

In response to the Christian argument that God made a new covenant with the Church which necessarily invalidates the old covenant with Israel, Rosenberg reported, some Jewish theologians were suggesting that "[b]oth are valid, and valid absolutely, one for Judaism the other for Christianity." This new theory pronounces both religions true.[41]

B. Zvi Sobel's survey of Christian missions to the Jews, "Jews and Christian Evangelization: The Anglo-American Approach," (1964), concluded that "conversions to Christianity have occurred in every age and in every environment within Christendom." He believed that there has never been a time in history when Christian missionary activity toward Jews has not been going on. He labels conversion statistics in this area as "impossibly unreliable."[42]

The Task Force on Missionary Activity of the Jewish Community Relations Council of New York commissioned David Berger and Michael Wyschogrod in 1978 to write a Jewish response to the Christian missionary approach to Jews and, especially, the relation of "Jewish Christianity" to Judaism. In a "Note to the Reader" in the book that resulted, *Jews and "Jewish Christianity,"* Berger and Wyschogrod wrote that the purpose of the book was twofold: "first to persuade Jews who have been attracted to "Jewish Christianity" to take another look; second, to familiarize other readers with a Jewish approach to what has become a controversial and hotly debated topic."[43]

Berger and Wyschogrod repeat the claim made by previous defenders of Judaism that "Judaism has never believed that everyone should become Jewish" and that "good people of all religions have a share in the world to come." They do assert that Judaism does believe that "Jews should be Jews and nothing else." While their book is designed to explain why Jews should remain in Judaism, it is not directed at non-Jews.[44]

The assumption is made by Berger and Wyschogrod that those Jews attracted to Christianity are sincere seekers after truth. They find it necessary to talk about the motives behind a Jew's interest in Christianity because for centuries "many Jews who converted to Christianity did so out of motives of self-interest rather than sincerity." As a result, they note, suspicion of motives for conversion became "deeply ingrained in the Jewish mind" until "many Jews find it hard to believe that a Jew who embraces Christianity can be sincere."[45]

As part of their effort to "retrieve" Jews from Christianity, Berger and Wyschogrod challenge some of the basic beliefs of Christianity which they find to be contrary to Jewish theology. Chief among them, quite naturally, is to dispute the messiahship of Jesus Christ. They use some of the arguments first brought forward by modernist Christian theologians to explain how the religion of Jesus became the Christianity of the New Testament. They argue that the followers of Jesus Christ were taken by surprise when He was crucified, forcing them to regroup and come up with some way to explain how the Messiah and Redeemer of Israel could have been destroyed. Rather than admit that they were wrong, that Jesus Christ was not the promised Messiah, Berger and Wyschogrod charge that the disciples claimed that Jesus had been resurrected, reinterpreted Bible texts to prove that the Messiah would be killed, forecasted His second coming to bring about world peace and changed the meaning of the first coming to atonement for original sin. "The basic structure of this explanation was to shift the function of the Messiah from a visible level, where it could be tested, to an invisible, where it could not," they concluded.[46]

Berger and Wyschogrod charge that "Jewish-Christians" distort the Old Testament by extracting "proof-texts" that "prove" that Jesus was the promised Messiah. If God wanted to teach the virgin birth, the trinity, the divinity of the Messiah, the crucifixion of the Messiah and other important ideas, they maintain, then He would have taught them "clearly and unambiguously to the Jews" and not so obscurely that they can be "discerned only by someone who already knows them to be true." Not only do Jewish scholars have a hard time finding proofs for Christian doctrines in the Old Testament, but so do many "modern Christian scholars." It is not possible, they declare, to "turn the Hebrew Bible into a Christian book. The Bible must therefore be read as it really is, as a purely Jewish work."[47]

The trend away from missions to the Jews by Christians is noted by Berger and Wyschogrod. "While there was a time when almost all Christian churches were engaged in missionizing Jews, in recent times," they state, "most churches have discontinued special efforts directed at Jews." One of the reasons for this, Berger and Wyschogrod find, is the "widespread conviction among many Christian thinkers that Judaism stands in a special relationship to Christianity and, therefore, that Jews cannot be addressed as people in need of salvation."[48] Encouraged by this development, they still remain intensely concerned about missions to the Jews, especially those efforts being conducted by "Jewish-Christians."

"Jewish-Christian" groups preach a "Jesus or damnation" theology. "Jews coming into contact with these groups are told that if they do not accept Jesus as their personal saviour, they are condemned to the tortures of everlasting hell since their sins cannot be forgiven," write Berger and Wyschogrod. Jews are also told by "Jewish-Christians" that "sin can be forgiven only by the shedding of blood, and since Judaism no longer practices sacrifice, it cannot bring about forgiveness of sin." This "Jewish-Christian" view of sin and forgiveness is contrasted by Berger and Wyschogrod with the Jewish belief in the infinite mercy of God in accepting the return to Him of all those who turn from sin in repentance, without a blood sacrifice being mandated.[49]

Berger and Wyschogrod make an earnest plea to Jews to reject the overtures of Gentile Christians and "Jewish-Christians" to convert to Christianity. They have concluded that Jews who become "Jewish-Christians" will be absorbed into the Gentile Christian community. For a Jew to choose "Jewish-Christianity" is to opt for the "dissolution of the people God wants to remain his eternal people."[50]

All Jews owe a debt to their ancestors for remaining true to the faith. Berger and Wyschogrod appeal to Jews contemplating conversion to remember that their ancestors often had to choose between death and baptism; therefore, they should not forsake the faith of their fathers so easily. Past martyrdom for the faith rather than conversion to Christianity "creates a special obligation for their descendants not to render that sacrifice meaningless." Jews are urged, before they abandon their ancient religion, to make an all-out effort to study, know and live Judaism. Berger and Wyschogrod remind their readers that Israel was chosen to be "a nation of priests and a holy people," and that by "remaining loyal to your people, you can help it to live up to its divine calling." In the postholocaust era, a Jew is called to remember the murdered 6 million and "to live a life worthy of their sacrifice." They are warned, "Your choice will determine not only your religious destiny but the identity of your descendants as well."[51]

Jewish opposition to Christian missionary efforts is presented in Gerald Sigal's book *The Jew and the Christian Missionary: A Jewish Response to Missionary Christianity* (1981). He writes in his introduction, "The entire missionary view of the Jewish relationship to God is fundamentally wrong." This view, Sigal charges, is based upon "prejudiced Christian theological appraisal of Judaism" and a misreading of the "essential meaning of the Torah." The Christian missionary starts, he notes, with the assumption that the Jewish Bible is God's revealed Word but that 2,000 years ago Judaism went astray and Christianity then became the "continuation of the Jewish spiritual past." In support of these claims the Christian missionary cannot attack the Hebrew Bible which is accepted as divinely inspired; therefore, "missionaries propose their own radically altered constructions of the meaning of biblical verses," which contradict the authentic teachings of ancient Israel.[52]

"The driving force behind the missionary movement's efforts against Judaism, Sigal finds, "is the conviction that the validity of Christianity requires the withering away of ancient Jewish practice and belief." Missionaries accomplish this, he argues, by attempting to "undermine the foundations of Judaism." Knowing that "[t]he survival of the Jewish people is directly conditioned upon the observance of the Torah," Sigal claims that the "missionary movement has consistently sought to destroy any meaningful adherence to the Torah by contending that its observance is no longer required by God." But, he contends, the missionary message that faith in Jesus replaced adherence to the Torah is refuted by the "religious experience of the Jewish people." For through prayer and observance of the laws of the Torah, he asserts, the Jewish people have "always enjoyed a direct and unmediated relationship with God."[53]

While Sigal maintains that he has not written his book "with malice nor with intent to insult either Christians or Christianity," it is written to set "aright those Jews who are being deluded into joining Christianity by out-and-out distortions of the Hebrew Bible." He does not seek to criticize those Christians who do not seek to convert the Jewish people.[54] However, he must defend Judaism against the assaults of the Christian missionary movement.

The main body of Sigal's book is a refutation of Christian missionary "reinterpretation" of the Hebrew Bible. Toward the end of the book he concludes, "No appeal to faith can alter the fact that the Scriptures do not teach what the missionaries preach. . . . Confronted with the inconsistencies of its contentions, the missionary movement claims that its beliefs are a matter of faith." He attacks this appeal to faith as an "apologetic device" used by missionaries to "stifle all criticism."[55]

"Disregarding the biblical word in favor of reliance on what is said to be faith, the missionary movement distorts the revelation of Sinai," Sigal claims, "presuming to know better than God what His intentions are for the people of Israel." He traces the "distortions" back to early Christianity, particularly to Paul, who extolled "faith in Jesus while deprecating the observance of the laws of the Torah." He calls Paul's denigration of the Law "actually only his own ideas and not those of God." The modern missionary movement, according to Sigal, "still follows the Pauline method of deceit and pretense. Its antirational faith-experience apology is an excuse in the face of the reality that the Jewish Scriptures do not show Jesus to be the Messiah."[56]

"The Jewish convert to Christianity has been deceived by subtle mental manipulation," Sigal argues, "into accepting Jesus as God, into thinking evil is righteousness, and into accepting the preposterous view that the observance of God's Law is against the will of God." Instead of relying on the faith founded on Scripture, he finds that converts base their Christian beliefs on a personal experience of Jesus in their lives. He categorically states that "[t]he belief that Jesus can affect one's life is irrational and biblically untenable. Convincing oneself that something is true does not make it so." Human history is full of sincere believers who trusted in false notions.[57]

Modern critics of the "Christian missions to the Jews" enterprise within the Jewish community claim, as did their forerunners, that missions to the pagan world by Christians are not objectionable to Jews, only efforts to convert the Jewish people. Samuel Levine writes in *You Take Jesus, I'll Take God: How to Refute Christian Missionaries* (1980) that he has nothing against Christian missionary efforts to convert pagans. "That is highly meritorious, because they are transforming an immoral, primitive person into a more moral and spiritual one. However," he maintains, "that is not true when a Jew becomes a Christian." While he has no ill will toward the majority of Christians, he seeks to challenge the "multi-million dollar effort on the part of the Christians to convert as many Jews as they can."[58]

Equally as critical of Christian missions to the Jews is Dov Aharoni Fisch's book *Jews for Nothing: On Cults, Intermarriage and Assimilation* (1984). Fisch writes:

> As vultures hovering and circling over thirsting bodies in the desert, they come with their tracts to the spiritual wastelands of suburbia, patiently waiting for the opportunity to snare yet another Jewish soul thirsting for divinity. They smile and softly preach the gospel of peace. Sometimes they wear buttons which proclaim "I Found It!" Other times they dress in shirts which read: "Jews for Jesus." They are Christian missionaries, and they will stop at nothing to win the soul of the young Jew.[59]

Fisch recalls that the missionary approach to the Jewish people by Christianity is nothing new. "Having been butchered by crusaders, burned by bishops, and defamed by leaders of all Christian denominations for our manifold 'crimes' (such as causing the Black Death by poisoning the wells of Europe, and killing Christian babies at Passover time), we have come to know the Christian missionaries," he declares. Further, he alleges, "They are in pursuit of our souls, and they will kill us if they have to, but only for the lofty purpose of saving us, of course." Even though the modern missionary comes preaching love, Fisch asserts, it does not take a yeshiva education to know that there is "more to

Christianity than 'love thy neighbor.' Two thousand years of crusades, inquisitions, pogroms, and holocausts are hard to cover up, even on Madison Avenue."[60]

"For a number of decades," writes Fisch, "Christian missionary groups had been racking their brains in efforts to conceive a tactic which would increase the rate of Jewish conversions. Labor as they might, they were unable to break the ice. Jews were just turned off to the entire Christian presentation." Missionaries tried everything, even "offering parents free room, board, clothing, and education for their children, in return for their souls." However, Fisch concludes, "while a few terribly pressured individuals gave in now and then, the overall missionary effort was a flop. Jews just wouldn't become Christians."[61]

Fisch was forced to admit that the "renewal of missionary fervor" in missions to the Jews could be attributed to a "new version of Christian proselytizing," which emphasized that Jews could maintain a tie with Judaism and still become Christians.[62] They could become "Jewish-Christians," "Messianic Jews," or "Jews for Jesus."

The first major ripple concerning evangelization among Jews in the last thirty years in America was the evangelistic campaign known as Key 73. Though nationwide in scope and involving many denominations, it did not specifically target Jewish people for conversion.

Jewish leaders noted the "surge of support from a wide range of conservative Christians" for the State of Israel in the early 1980s. Rabbi Marc Tanenbaum of the American Jewish Committee remarked, "The evangelical community is the largest and fastest growing block of pro-Israeli, pro-Jewish sentiment in the country." The Orthodox Rabbi Alexander Schindler challenged this evangelical support of Jews: "Even their support of Israel is intrinsically demeaning to Jews," since it is tied to an "ingathering" of Jews to Israel before there can be a Second Coming of Christ.[63] This political/prophetic interest did not preclude continued evangelization among the Jewish people.

Messianic Jewish congregations have begun to spread across America, notes Mike Masch of the University of Pennsylvania, in the mid-1980s. This interest is related "to the coming of age of a Jewish baby-boom generation that was more independent of its parents and more ignorant than any that had come before." Messianic Judaism angers Rabbi Stephen Robbins of the Los Angeles Task Force on Missionary Efforts. He calls it "an attempt to supplant the existing Jewish community by redefining Judaism, with Messianic Jewish groups creating their own synagogues, co-opting traditional Jewish symbols and superimposing their own theology." An anti-Hebrew Christian group countering "Jews for Jesus" has been started called "Jews for Judaism."[64]

In May of 1989, "Fifteen evangelical Protestant theologians issued a statement warning that creating a dialogue with Jews cannot substitute for converting them. The theologians urge Christian churches to put a high priority on proselytism." Rabbi A. James Rudin, of the American Jewish Committee, "denounced the evangelicals' statement, saying it portrayed an 'exhausted Judaism fit only to be replaced by the authors' own evangelical brand of Christianity.' " The statement by the evangelicals describes Jews as "branches of God's olive tree" that have "broken off." The theologians deny that contemporary Judaism "contains within itself true knowledge of God's salvation." While defending Jews becoming Christians it rejected "coercive or deceptive proselytizing."[65]

"Asserting that Jews 'need [Jesus] as much as anyone else,' more than 4,000 leaders of evangelical Protestantism worldwide, meeting here [Manila], reaffirmed their determination to continue to evangelize the Jewish people," it was reported in July of 1989. Adopted by the Lausanne International Congress, the manifesto "specifically rejected the belief of most liberal Christians that because Jews have their own covenant with God, they should not be pressed to convert to Christianity." The declaration stated clearly, "we therefore reject the thesis that Jews have their own covenant which renders faith in Jesus unnecessary."[66]

At a conference of Christians and Jews held in Sherman Oaks, California in May of 1992, there was agreement on support of Israel and fighting anti-Semitism, but "one sticky issue" was unresolved, "evangelistic tactics that target Jews for conversion." Rabbi A. James Rudin, of the American Jewish Committee, noted that most American Jewish leaders "respect Billy Graham because the evangelist offers his Gospel message to everyone. . . . What we object to are missions, specialized ministries, campaigns and booklets that target Jews qua Jews to convert to Christianity."[67]

The Southern Baptist Convention (SBC) became more intensely involved in Jewish evangelism in recent years, although they have maintained a witness among Jews in America on and off for many years. In 1996 at their annual meeting the SBC passed a resolution which called for the 15.6-million-member denomination to "direct our energies and resources toward the proclamation of the Gospel to the Jews." At the same meeting the Home Mission Board appointed a missionary to American Jews, a post that had been vacant for eight years.[68]

Larry Lewis, president of the Home Mission Board, rejected the two-covenant view held by many interfaith Protestants. Lewis said, "We deny that position and we denounce that position. We believe that all people need a personal vital relationship with Jesus Christ." Pointing out that "Southern Baptists had passed 10 resolutions since 1867 encouraging evangelizing the Jews" this one was "singled out" to be construed as anti-Semitic by Jewish and interfaith groups. Noting that the resolution "undermines" the movement toward interfaith acceptance, Rabbi Eric Yoffie, president of the Union of American Hebrew Congregations, stated, "It seems to us that this is a direct attack on the Jewish religious tradition."[69]

Defending the resolution, Dr. R. Philip Roberts, director of the Interfaith Witness Department of the Home Mission Board of the SBC, noted that, "the resolution itself was the result of a growing and influential number of Messianic believers and congregations within the SBC, who were chagrined by the fact that 'our evangelistic efforts have largely neglected the Jewish people.' "[70]

Resolution 10, passed by the SBC meeting in New Orleans in June, 1996, dealt specifically with Jewish evangelism. It notes, among other things, neglect of Jewish evangelism at home and abroad, indebtedness to the Jewish people for "the Scriptures, and our Savior, the Messiah of Israel," denial that Jewish people do not need the gospel, a growing responsiveness among Jews to the gospel, the need for prayer and a direction of resources "toward the proclamation of the gospel to the Jewish people."[71]

Rabbi Jonathan S. Woll, of Temple Avoda in Fair Lawn, New Jersey reacted to the 1996 SBC resolution this way: "I appreciate the sense of commitment and intensity of conviction obvious in the Southern Baptist Convention's Resolution on Jewish Evangelism. However, its theological position, with one of its assumptions that Jews live in sin, is a challenge to civility, to the sense of how citizens in the United States should treat each other." Woll continued his criticism of the resolution by saying that it

> . . . seriously breaches the relatively recent trust that
> many American religious communities have built up

since the Holocaust, the ultimate attempt to eradicate Jews from history and future existence. Obviously, the Southern Baptist Convention can envision a world without Jews. I can only envision a world with Jews believing in the ever-living God, an expectation based on a sacrosanct promise made years ago, renewed daily by Jews through prayer, faith, and deed.[72]

The SBC published material in 1999 to prepare their members to evangelize Jewish people. "The booklet, produced by the Southern Baptist International Mission Board, was sent to 40,000 U.S. churches to coincide with Rosh Hashana, the Jewish new year, which starts 10 days of reflection that end Sept. 20 with Yom Kippur, the faith's Day of Atonement." The material "offers a thumbnail guide to Judaism and suggests special prayers for the souls of Jews." It also encourages Baptists to "befriend Jewish neighbors as a step toward converting them."[73]

Objecting to the 1999 SBC prayer guides and Baptist participation in conferences on Jewish Evangelism, Philip D. Abramowitz, director of the Task Force on Missionaries and Cults, said he found this disturbing primarily because it "promotes the misuse of our most sacred themes and symbols to the cause of conversion." He called on the denomination "to repent of its embrace of deceptive tactics." Abramowitz felt the need to "educate our community better," adding, "we have to really make our community aware around the world that they are targets" of missionaries.[74]

It is clear that the SBC prayer guides have struck a raw nerve in the Jewish community. "It is pure arrogance for any one religion to assume that they hold the truth," says Abraham Foxman, national director of the Anti-Defamation League. "The call to prayer among Southern Baptists is doubly offensive and disrespectful in light of the High Holidays."[75]

Of particular concern to Jews is Messianic Judaism and its growth in America. "In New York, Jewish organizations have asserted that Southern Baptist approaches to Jews involve deception, because the denomination increasingly supports messianic Jewish groups, which say one can be fully Jewish while also believing in Jesus as the Messiah."[76]

Nearly every evangelistic denomination involved in Jewish evangelism, including the Alliance and independent Jewish mission boards in North America, has adopted the "fulfilled Jew" approach to reaching the Jewish people over the last twenty to thirty years. The old style of Jewish evangelism which turned converted Jews into "Gentile Christians" has been abandoned for the far more successful method pioneered by "Jews For Jesus" and others. This change has only angered the Jewish community more. They seem merely to want most to be left alone in their beliefs.

As long as Paul's words in Romans 10:1-4 are in the inerrant Word of God, there seems to be no end in sight to the objections raised by the Jewish community against missionary efforts among their people:

> Brothers, my heart's desire and prayer to God for the Israelites is that they may be saved. For I can testify about them that they are zealous for God, but their zeal is not based on knowledge. Since they did not know the righteousness that comes from God and sought to establish their own, they did not submit to God's righteousness. Christ is the end of the law so that there may be righteousness for everyone who believes.

Endnotes

1. A.B. Simpson, *Christ in the Bible Vol. XVII: Romans* (New York: Christian Alliance Publishing, 1904), 65.

2. A.B. Simpson, *The Gospel of the Kingdom* (New York: Christian Alliance Publishing, 1890), 167-172.

3. Ibid., 173-183.

4. *Sixth Annual Report of the International Missionary Alliance* (New York: The International Missionary Alliance, 1893),18-19.

5. Isaac M. Wise, *A Defense of Judaism Versus Proselytizing Christianity* (Cincinnati: The American Israelite, 1889), 8-9.

6. Ibid., 9.

7. Ibid., 12-13.

8. Ibid., 121-122, 124.

9. Solomon Schindler, *Messianic Expectations* (Boston: Index Association, 1885), 4-5.

10. Ibid., 7.

11. A.M. Radin, "Helping the Fallen," *The American Hebrew*, January 20, 1893: 394.

12. Editorial, *The American Hebrew*, Nov. 15, 1895: 37.

13. Editorial, *The American Hebrew*, Feb. 10, 1893: 481-482.

14. Editorial, *The American Hebrew*, Feb. 10, 1893, 481.

15. Minnie D. Louis, "Mission Work Among the Unenlightened Jews," *The American Hebrew*, Sept. 15, 1893: 625.

16. Editorial, *The American Hebrew*, Aug. 2, 1895: 305.

17. Editorial, *The American Hebrew*, Dec. 20, 1895: 198.

18. Editorial, "Work to Be Done," *The American Hebrew*, Nov. 29, 1896: 98.

19. Editorial, *The American Hebrew*, June 1, 1894: 139.

20. Louis Weiss, *Some Burning Questions: An Exegetical Treatise on the Christianizing of Judaism* (Columbus, OH: n.p., 1893), 5.

21. Ibid., 5, 8.

22. Ibid., 17.

23. Ibid., 12, 15.

24. B. Felsenthal, *Why Do the Jews Not Accept Jesus as Their Messiah?* (Chicago: Bloch & Newman, 1893), 3.

25. Ibid., 5-6.

26. Ibid., 18-19.

27. Ibid., 22.

28. Lewis Hart, *A Jewish Reply to Christian Evangelists* (New York: Bloch Publishing, 1906), iv.

29. Ibid., v, ix.

30. Ibid., 2-3.

31. Ibid., 30, 164.

32. Nathan Solomon Joseph, *Why I Am Not a Christian: A Reply to the Conversionists* (London: Jewish Religious Union for the Advancement of Liberal Judaism, 1908), 1-16.

33. Louis Wirth, *The Ghetto* (Chicago: Univ. of Chicago Press, 1928), 37.

34. Ibid., 260-261.

35. Trude Weiss-Rosmarin, *Judaism and Christianity* (New York: The Jewish Book Club, 1943), 15, 54, 58, 86, 91, 103, 109, 118, 125.

36. Hyman B. Grinstein, *The Rise of the Jewish Community of New York 1654-1860* (Philadelphia: The Jewish Publication Society of America, 1945), 382-384, 585.

37. Ibid., 384-385.

38. Ibid., 384.

39. Ibid., 381-387.

40. Stuart E. Rosenberg, *America Is Different: The Search for Jewish Identity* (New York: The Burning Bush Press, 1964), 35, 36, 136.

41. Ibid., 120.

42. B. Zvi Sobel, "Jews and Christian Evangelization: The Anglo-American Approach," *American Jewish Historical Quarterly* Dec. 1968: 242.

43. David Berger and Michael Wyschogrod, *Jews and "Jewish Christianity"* (Philadelphia: KTAV Publishing House, Inc., 1978), 9.

44. Ibid., 12-13.

45. Ibid., 13.

46. Ibid., 14.

47. Ibid., 34-37, 51.

48. Ibid., 52.

49. Ibid., 53, 59.

50. Ibid., 65-66.

51. Ibid., 67-69.

52. Gerald Sigal, *The Jew and the Christian Missionary: A Jewish Response to Missionary Christianity* (New York: KTAV Publishing House, 1981), xv.

53. Ibid., xvi-xvii.

54. Ibid., xvii-xviii.

55. Ibid., 289.

56. Ibid., 289-290.

57. Ibid., 290-291.

58. Samuel Levine, *You Take Jesus, I'll Take God: How to Refute Christian Missionaries* (Los Angeles: Hamorah Press, 1980), 12.

59. Dov Aharoni Fisch, *Jews for Nothing: On Cults, Intermarriage and Assimilation* (New York: Feldsheim Publishers, 1984), 21.

60. Ibid., 21-23.

61. Ibid., 23.

62. Ibid.

63. Richard Bernstein, "Evangelicals Strengthening Bonds with Jews," *The New York Times*, Section 1, Part 1, p. 1; Lexus Nexus. 3/8/00.

64. Russell Chandler, "Traditional Jews on Attack to Shelter Flock from Messianics' Influence," *Los Angeles Times*, October 19, 1985, Part 2, p. 4: Lexus Nexus. 3/8/00.

65. Peter Steinfels, "Evangelical Group Urges Conversion of Jews," *The New York Times*, May 21, 1989, Section 1, Part 1, p. 37: Lexus Nexus. 3/8/00.

66. "Leaders at Manila Determined to Evangelize Jewish People," *The Washington Post*, July 29, 1989, p. C11: Lexus Nexus. 3/8/00.

67. John Dart, "Christian Leaders Discuss Evangelistic Conversion Tactics," *Los Angeles Times*, May 23, 1992, Part B, p. 4: Lexus Nexus. 3/8/00.

68. Laurie Goodstein, "Southern Baptist Support Resolution to Convert Jews; Move Seen as 'A Great Setback' for Interfaith Dialogue," *The Washington Post*, June 15, 1996, A Section, p. A02: Lexus Nexus. 3/8/00.

69. Ibid.

70. Rev. Dr. R. Philip Roberts, "Southern Baptists: We Must Lovingly Share Our Message with All," *The (Bergen) Record*, July 17, 1996, p. R02: Lexus Nexus: 3/8/00.

71. Ibid.

72. Rabbi Jonathan S. Woll, "Rabbi: Evangelism Challenges Civility, Denies Jews Link with God," *The (Bergen) Record*, July 17, 1996, p. R02; Lexus Nexus: 3/8/00.

73. Thomas Nord and Leslie Scanlon, "Prayer Guide Is Sent to Churches to Coincide with Rosh Hashana, Baptists Start Drive to Convert Jews," *The Courier-Journal* (Louisville, KY), September 10, 1999, p. 01a; Lexus Nexus. 3/8/00.

74. Gustav Niebuhr, "Baptists' Evangelism Concerns Jews," *The New York Times*, September 25, 1999, Section A, p. 9; Lexus Nexus. 3/8/00

75. Keith Hinson, "To the Jew First," *Christianity Today*, November 15, 1999, p.18; Lexus Nexus. 3/8/00.

76. Gustav Niebuhr, "Baptists' Ardor for Evangelism Angers Some Jews and Hindus," *The New York Times*, December 4, 1999, Section A, Page 10; Lexus Nexus. 3/8/00.

Premillennialism in the
Medieval and Reformation Times

Harold P. Shelly

For many, Y2K fatigue is already a thing of the past, almost medieval; it is like something out of the Dark Ages. Yet the idea of a New Age of peace and justice, which existed in those times, lives on. During tough times, people yearn for the *parousia* of peace and justice. Whenever political and social conditions become unbearable, people look for a deliverer, a messiah who will come and set the captives free. This was certainly true during the medieval and Reformation periods.[1]

Two outlooks toward a millennium dominate medieval and Reformation thinking. The first of these, articulated by Augustine of Hippo, is usually called amillennialism. The second is millennialism or chiliasm. The most significant exponent of the latter is Joachim of Fiore in the twelfth century. Immediately one is struck with an incongruity. Augustine wrote on the subject in the early fifth century, much earlier than Joachim. Augustine himself was not ignorant of a chiliastic strain, but he determined to eradicate it. Still, it lived on. This strain was maintained throughout the early medieval period by many who cherished the Apocalypse of John and embraced the so-called Sibylline Oracles. Whereas Augustine's viewpoint became the official viewpoint of the organized church, the Chiliasts tended to be the outsiders.

Medieval millennialism was often part and parcel of protest movements. Its adherents were usually the downtrodden masses. While the institutional church preached apostolic poverty, in practice it accumulated great wealth. Too often its prelates lived in luxury while they taxed the poor to support their extravagant lifestyle. Thus millennialism had an anti-institutional impulse. Crop failures, famine, death from plagues, conflicts between church and state, and warfare between noble families haunted the populace. Feudal laws made to protect the peasant population were gradually altered to the injury of the poor. It was as if the Four Horsemen of the Apocalypse—conquest, famine, wars and death—incessantly rode roughshod over medieval Europe. The Crusades against the infidel Turk provided another backdrop for misery and a model for the peasants. Whereas nobility went on their crusades into the Middle East to rescue the Holy Land from the infidel Turk, peasants went on shepherd crusades against faithless churchmen and nobility to create a Holy Land in Europe. False prophets recurrently arose and led people, usually into greater misery. Now back to Augustine.

Aurelius Augustine of Hippo and Millennialism

Augustine of Hippo (354-430), an African, was born in Tagaste and later served the Church in Hippo, located in modern-day Algeria. Indisputably he was the major, definitive theologian of the Latin west. His mother, Monica, a believer, tried to bring him up as a Christian, but his father, Patricius, an unbeliever, won the early days. In his quest for truth he first joined the dualistic Manichaean sect; later he adhered to Neo-Platonic dualism. After a long search for certainty which took him to Rome and Milan, he experienced a decisive conversion in the year A.D. 386. The same year the Goths entered the Empire, Augustine entered the Church; he was then thirty-two years of age. Doubtless a genius, his thinking touches almost all the doctrines of Western Christianity. In influence he ranks only behind Paul and Jesus. At the time of the Protestant Reformation, Calvin, Luther and the Catholics all referred to him more than anyone else. Thus, his views on the millennium are of great significance for all of Christendom.

Barbarian intrusion into the Roman Empire increased and non-Christian writers blamed the Christians. In *City of God*, Augustine's answer to the critics, he sets forth his philosophy (or theology) of history. For him there are two cities recognized by their two loves. Those whose love is holy and good are in the City of God. Those whose love is impure, whose love is for earthly things are outside the City of God (*City of God*, IV - 3). It is not, as some pagan writers allege, because of Rome's acceptance of the Christian faith, rather the Romans got what they deserved. Rome was not the city of God. In his *City of God*, among other concepts Augustine advanced the following ideas related to history and the kingdom of God:

> 1. History has at its beginning the creation, its center in Christ, and, as its consummation, the judgment and transformation of all things.

> 2. Because God has foreknowledge, he knew that man would be misdirected and evil would thereby come into the world, but he also knew that through His grace good could be brought from evil.

> 3. History is divided into two cities formed by alternative loves: the earthly city by the love of self, and the heavenly city by the love of God.[2]

Augustine was aware of millennialism, to which many still adhered in spite of repudiation by theologians like Origen.[3] In fact, he implies that he once was a millennialist. Some, he asserts, are enthralled with the idea of a thousand years. In reference to Peter's words (2 Peter 3:8, KJV), "one day is with the Lord as a thousand years, and a thousand years as one day," they imagine that "there should follow on the completion of six thousand years, as of six days, a kind of seventh-day Sabbath in the succeeding thousand years." He notes, "for I myself, too, once held this opinion." He continues, "they assert that those who then rise again shall enjoy the leisure of immoderate carnal banquets." "They who do believe them are called by the spiritual [those who reject the notions of a "carnal" millennium] Chiliasts, which we may literally reproduce by the name Millenarians." To refute this is "a tedious process" he adds. So he proceeds to show how Revelation 20:1-6 should be understood rather than refuting the Millenarians.[4]

So then, how does Augustine explain the thousand-year reference in Revelation? Quite easily, he thinks. John simply "used the thousand years as an equivalent for the whole duration of this world, employing the number of perfection to mark the fulness of time."[5] He continues, "[A] thousand is the cube of ten. For ten times ten makes a hundred, that is, the square on a plane. But to give this height, and make it a cube, the hundred is again multiplied by ten, which gives a thousand."[6] Clever! That which John speaks of is the interval between the first and second coming "which goes by the name of a thousand years." At the end of this indefinite period the devil is loosed for three years and six months and the saints are sheltered although "the Almighty does not absolutely seclude the saints from his temptation, but shelters only their inner man, where faith resides, that by outward temptation they may grow in grace."[7] Clearly he does not accept the notion of an earthly thousand-year reign of Christ on earth following a period of tribulation. But while the church is expanding, the devil is bound.

At the end of this thousand years, the devil seduces the nations to battle against the "camp of the saints . . . and the beloved city" (Revelation 20:7-10, KJV). This, says Augustine, is when the devil unleashes savage persecution against the church: "the whole city of God is assailed by the whole city of the devil, as each exists on the earth."[8] The camp is "the Church of Christ extending over the whole world." So that wherever the Church is in the whole world, "there it shall be encompassed by savage persecution of all its enemies . . . that is, it shall be straitened, and hard pressed, and shut up in the straits of tribulation, but shall not desert its military duty, which is signified by the word 'camp.' "[9]

Thus, Augustine set the stage for medieval doctrine in his denial of a literal thousand-year reign of Christ on earth after the Second Coming. Instead, the thousand years is a figurative number for the period between the resurrection of Christ and the second coming of Christ. This period he also calls the kingdom of Christ or the kingdom of heaven and the age of the church. The case is settled for Augustine, who "articulated this position, and it became the dominant interpretation in medieval times. His teaching was so fully accepted that at the Council of Ephesus in 431, belief in the millennium was condemned as superstitious."[10] This sounds so final, but millennialism could not be so easily discarded.

The Sibylline Oracles

If the Fathers at Ephesus thought their anathema would eliminate millennialism, they were sadly mistaken. Circulating throughout the medieval period was a collection of prophetic writings known as the Sibylline Oracles. In ancient Greece people called upon a sibyl, a female prophet, to reveal the future. Collections of these predictions were esteemed in pagan society. Not to be outdone, it seems that Jews and Christians produced their own "oracles," but pretended them to be utterances of Greek sibyls who made prophecies that should lead the non-believer to the truth. The collection of Sibylline Oracles consists of fifteen books. Book seven includes eschatological prophecies. Some sections are clearly pagan, some are Jewish and others are of Christian origin or Christian interpolation.[11] The fourth-century Christian apologist, Lactantius, used the Erythraean sibyl, which is favorably quoted by Augustine in his *City of God*.[12] The prophecy is arranged in such a way that the initial letters—twenty-seven (3 × 3 × 3) letters—of each line spells out in Greek, *Jesus Christ of-God Son Savior*. Augustine seems to use this sibyl uncritically. So it was that the Sibylline Oracles could be used by the medieval church with the implicit approval of the great Church Father Augustine.

For many, these oracles substantiated the Apocalypse of John. The conquering Christ of the Book of Revelation was the hero. In the Sibylline literature the hero was an emperor type allegedly predicted by Greek prophets.[13] Cohn contends, "Throughout the Middle Ages the Sibylline eschatology persisted alongside the eschatologies derived from the Book of Revelation, influencing them and being influenced by them but generally surpassing them in popularity."[14] These were widely studied and interpreted to reflect contemporary situations. Bad times were foretold; enemies were described as Antichrist and the heroes were Christ-figures or persons immediately preparing the way for Christ's return in judgment. And the oracles and the Apocalypse allegedly predicted them all. Thus, for many centuries, primitive premillennialism, based on the Apocalypse and the Sibylline Oracles, continued to bolster millennial expectations. A more fully developed millennialism would wait for Joachim of Fiore.

Joachim of Fiore

The major exponent of millennialism in the latter Middle Ages was Joachim Fiore (c. 1132-1202).[15] In his system he developed the idea of three ages or dispensations. These are the successive ages of: (1) the Father, (2) the Son and (3) the Holy Spirit, or (1) Law, (2) Grace and (3) "Ecclesia Spiritualis," the age of the Spiritual Church. The latter was to begin about 1260. On the basis of a generation being about thirty years and the generations from Abraham to Jesus being forty-two generations according to Matthew (1:17), Joachim reasoned that the time from the birth of Christ to the return of Christ must also be forty-two generations. Thus, about 1260 years after the birth of Jesus Christ, the age of the Son would be completed and the age of the Holy Spirit would begin. The step from this 1260 years into the thousand years of the Apocalypse (Revelation 20:2-7) was easy.[16] Before this Spiritual age, new religious orders would convert the whole world and bring on the new age of the Spirit.

Joachim "identified the resulting new vision with that 'everlasting gospel' which, according to the Book of Revelation, is to be preached to all peoples in the Last Days. . . . Half a century after Joachim's death, 'evangelium aeternum' had become the slogan of a widespread messianic movement."[17] This evangelium aeternum referred to in Revelation 14:6 contains the only use of the word gospel (ευαγγελιον) in the Apocalypse. In Revelation 14 John speaks of 144,000 who stand before the throne in constant praise. They are said to be unmarried or virgins (παρθενοι). Joachim seems to picture them as a vast monastery of celibate monks singing in ecstacy until the judgment day.[18]

This new paradigm of Joachim gained the ascendancy among millennialists in the latter part of the Middle Ages. Franciscan Spirituals saw themselves as the fulfillment of the prophecy. It is even possible that the Franciscan and Dominican orders were originally approved to keep the fervor of Joachimites under the control of the Church hierarchy. Later Franciscan Spirituals became a thorn in the side of the papacy.[19] Moreover, the new paradigm ran counter to the officially accepted Augustinian view of the millennium.

> Joachim's idea of the third age was of course wholly unreconcilable with the Augustinian view that the Kingdom of God had been realized, so far as it ever could be realized on this earth, at that moment when the Church came into being and that there never would be any Millennium but this. In sponsoring Joachim the Papacy was therefore—quite unwittingly—sanctioning a new form of that chiliasm which for centuries it had been condemning as heretical.[20]

Joachim's new order would supersede the Papacy. In the Age of the Spirit, the Church of the Spirit would no longer need the clergy; even written Scriptures would be unnecessary.

If the papacy, by approving the new mendicant orders and disciplining the Spirituals, could contain the millennial fever in the thirteenth century, the late fourteenth and fifteenth centuries would be more difficult. England and France would be involved in prolonged warfare called the Hundred Years War, and the Papacy would endure the Babylonian Captivity and the Great Schism. England would favor one pope; France, the other. A peasant girl, Joan of Arc, would hear voices and lead French armies to victory. An Oxford theologian, John Wyclif, would send out his disciples to proclaim a new gospel throughout England. An academic dean in Prague, John Huss, would preach against the evils of the Church. All of these would be declared heretical. Joan of Arc and John Huss would be burned at the stake. In the case of Huss, his followers resisted and the Hussite wars ensued. Again, many saw imminent judgment and the millennium on the horizon.

Taborite Millennialism

Followers of Huss desired both bread and wine in holy communion. Within the Hussite movement were the so-called Utraquists, a more moderate group, who returned to the Catholic Church when their demand for "communion in both kinds" *(sub Utraque specie)* was granted. More radical Taborites who had their center on a mountain which they renamed Mount Tabor, from which they were called Taborites, continued the struggle against their adversaries. The crusade, which began among the common people and was led by members of the trade guilds, continued to lure adherents. That they named their fortified garrison south of Prague Mount Tabor is not insignificant.[21] Many believed that Mount Tabor between Nazareth and Tiberius was the setting of Jesus' transfiguration. Some also supposed it was the place of the ascension. Several centuries before the Taborites, Crusaders had built a church on Mount Tabor. Now the Taborites were on a new crusade to purify the land and bring in the new age. Purification would precede the Second Coming and the millennium.

The Holy Roman Emperor Sigismund, who after 1420 was also King of Bohemia, gathered a large army to suppress the Taborite movement. The Taborites fought back. "The afflictions now descending on Bohemia, the chiliastic Taborites recognized as the long-expected 'messianic woes'; and the conviction gave them a new militancy."[22] Now they went on the attack against all those they considered evil. Atrocities abounded on both sides. "But what can be said is that it was only amongst the Taborites that massacre was seen as a way of clearing the way for the Millennium."[23] As soon as they cleansed the land, the Lord would return and they would meet Him in the air. Together they would celebrate the messianic banquet on Mount Tabor and the Millennium, the Third Age of Joachim, would begin. Alas, fanaticism followed and not the *parousia*. Although the Taborite movement was wiped out in the battle of Lipany in 1434, Taborite propaganda continued to circulate throughout Europe. Peasants in the German towns bordering on Bohemia continued to harbor chiliastic expectations.

Though many peasant crusades sprang up in various parts of Germany, the most notorious was that led by Thomas Müntzer, a sometime visitor to Prague. As Norman Cohn delightfully segues:

> And meanwhile in a different part of Germany—
> Thuringia, always so fertile in chiliastic myths and
> movements—Thomas Müntzer was embarking on the
> stormy career which was to end by making him into a
> prophet of the egalitarian Millennium, and one whose
> fame has endured to the present day.[24]

The close of the fifteenth century had seen considerable discontent among peasants, whose lot in life was degenerating as they fell deeper into serfdom. Germany was seething religiously, economically and socially. Many hoped the emperor would lead them against the repressive princes of the realm; this did not happen. When the peasants heard Martin Luther proclaim that the Christian is a free person in Christ, they concluded they had found a new champion. They were wrong. Luther might understand their plight, but he would not condone rebellion. For him freedom was spiritual, not social or political. When the peasant wars came to Germany in the 1520s, Thomas Müntzer, not Martin Luther, was their champion.

Thomas Müntzer and the Peasant Kingdom

Thomas Müntzer became a follower of Luther shortly after Luther published his *Ninety-five Theses*. In 1519 Luther recommended Müntzer to be pastor of the church in Zwickau. Here Müntzer came in contact with Nicholas Storch, a weaver who had visited nearby Bohemia and absorbed Taborite doctrines. These he passed on to Müntzer. Later Müntzer himself would travel to Prague to connect with the Hussites. In his "Prague Manifesto" he predicts, "God will do marvelous things with his elect, especially in this country. For here the new Church will arise."[25] Without employing explicit millennial wording, Müntzer predicted the kingdom of the elect that the Taborites had fought to bring to their land. The millennium was near, "to be preceded by the ascendency of the Turk as Antichrist."[26] Müntzer also admitted indebtedness to the tradition of Joachim of Fiore.[27]

If Luther preferred the Psalms and the Epistles, Müntzer preferred Daniel and the Apocalypse. In them he found a radical social program: the kingdom of God would come to earth through the elect. Müntzer preached to the princes using Daniel and Revelation. Christ would destroy "the last of the kingdoms of this world, the imperial-papal monarchy" predicted by Daniel. Müntzer urged the princes to join with Christ and His elect, the stone which destroyed the image. The princes did not support Müntzer's program. When the princes rejected his beckoning, Müntzer joined the peasants on the road to revolution.[28] Chiliasts saw things in the Word which Luther, who urged the princes to have no part in chiliastic schemes and social revolution, could not imagine.[29]

In Allstedt Müntzer threw his lot in with the oppressed peasants. He would lead the saints into the new age of peace, justice and equality. In the terrible Peasants' Wars which ravaged Germany from 1524 to 1525, the princes were at first taken by surprise. But they soon regrouped and unleashed their full fury on the peasants and their supporters. Thomas Müntzer was apprehended in Frankenhausen and put to torture. Although he recanted his teachings, he was beheaded. The princes thus notified the peasants not to withstand earthly authority. This should have ended peasant attempts to establish the kingdom on earth, but it did not end. Eschatological hopes ignited by apocalyptic texts and fiery preaching cannot easily be extinguished. Other Chiliasts kept the promise alive in the volatile days in which they were living. In 1529 the plague again hit central Europe, the price of grain increased and additional taxes were levied on the peasants to support the war against the Turks. The condition of the peasants continued to deteriorate.

Both Luther and Müntzer believed that they were living in the last days and that the kingdom was imminent.

Just as much as Müntzer, Luther performed all his deeds in the conviction that the Last Days were at hand. But in his view the sole enemy was the Papacy, in which he saw Antichrist, the false prophet. It was by the dissemination of the true Gospel that the papacy would be overcome. When the task had been accomplished, Christ would return to pass sentence of eternal damnation upon the pope and his followers and to found a Kingdom—but a Kingdom which would not be of this world.[30]

Müntzer believed the elect needed to war against the evil of the church and state; Luther saw their rebellion as utterly evil. For Luther, the preaching of the eternal gospel would bring in the kingdom, but not an earthly kingdom.

The Diet of Speier

A frustrated Catholic emperor attempting to enforce conformity on all his subjects called the Imperial Diet to meet at Speier in the spring of 1529. The princes who followed Luther resisted his pressure and issued a protestation. Henceforth these protesters and their followers would be known as "Protestants."[31]

At that same session all the princes, Catholic and Protestant, agreed together to revive an ancient Justinian law against rebaptism. Henceforth in the Holy Roman Empire those who rebaptized others or refused to baptize infants—commonly branded "Anabaptists"—were forthwith guilty of a capital crime. This became a convenient way of dealing with all those outside the Catholic and Lutheran systems. Those who advocated millennialism antithetical to the dogma received from Augustine whether they baptized or not could easily receive the same label. Even the most peaceful Anabaptist became the object of persecution. The most notorious Anabaptist kingdom was in the city of Münster.

Melchior Hoffmann and the New Jerusalem

Meanwhile, as peaceful Swiss Anabaptists were fleeing persecution in Zurich and spreading out in southern Germany, Austria and Alsace, a new "Anabaptist" movement appeared in the Netherlands and northwestern Germany. The leader who gave his name to the northern movements was Melchior Hoffmann, a furrier by trade. He had been influenced by Martin Luther and had carried Lutheran teachings along the Baltic to Denmark and into the Netherlands. Not a thoroughgoing Lutheran, he held the same view of the sacrament as Zwingli and, like some of Zwingli's disciples, also came to question infant baptism. Initially Melchior did not advocate rebaptism for adult believers; he urged his followers to "stand still," to wait and not antagonize the civil authorities. Later in Strassburg, along the Rhine, he accepted believer's baptism. The Rhineland had long been a haunt for Chiliasts. Melchior preached "the imminence of the Second Coming and the Millennium" which was "to begin after a period of 'messianic woes'" in the year 1533 "the fifteenth centenary of the death of Christ."[32]

Melchiorites

The followers of Melchior Hoffmann multiplied rapidly in the Netherlands, where they became known as Melchiorites. His teachings, like those of Thomas Müntzer, had an apocalyptic bent; he predicted the kingdom of God would come to Strassburg about 1533 or 1534.[33] On his fourth visit to the city, the authorities put him into prison where he gladly waited for the coming kingdom. He spent the remainder of his life in a dungeon while the movement went on without him.

The Münster Fiasco

Many followers of Melchior now concluded that the promised kingdom was to be in another location, the episcopal city of Münster beyond the Rhineland, in Westphalia. Münster was founded in 800 by Charlemagne for his newly appointed bishop of the Saxons. In the sixteenth century Münster was the seat of a prince-bishop who seemed to care little for spiritual matters. In 1530 he attempted to sell his bishopric. Lutheran emissaries convinced the citizens to reform their city. Berndt (Bernhard) Rothmann, preaching assistant at St. Mauritz, led the assault on the old church. When the town council came to his support, the prince-bishop fled. The city was divided. Some adhered to the Zwinglian covenantal understanding of the sacrament, but others supported a more Lutheran approach to the sacraments. The division provided an opening for the chiliastic Melchiorites.

Presuming that Münster was now the place where they could establish the kingdom of God, Melchiorites began to arrive from the Netherlands. They persuaded Rothmann to accept their baptism. The bishop, meanwhile, began to organize a siege of the city, and non-Anabaptists fled the city. The Melchiorites invited other "Anabaptists" to join their new apocalyptic kingdom. On February 23, 1534, they won the town council and Jan Matthijs, a militant Melchiorite, arrived in Münster. Rothmann was reduced to the role of propagandist and matters deteriorated. Their invitation to all Anabaptists in other towns to join them suggested that Münster was a "blend of chiliasm and primitivism."[34]

When the prince-bishop and his Protestant allies tightened the siege, John of Leyden proclaimed himself messiah and initiated a "Davidic" kingdom which would spread over the whole world. As conditions deteriorated and more men were killed in skirmishes around the city, polygamy was sanctioned in the city. The imagined kingdom of God had become a kingdom of fools. In 1535 the city fell to the prince-bishop and its fanatical rulers were executed. Peasants must not take a city; see how they rule![35] For generations the tragic fiasco of Münster was used as an example of what these Anabaptists would do if they were not suppressed. Scorned along with the city was any thoughtful consideration of millennialism. All such discourse was unsafe as well as unorthodox. Most Anabaptists returned to the peaceful path to the kingdom of God—awaiting, but not executing, God's judgment.

At this point the observation of Robert G. Clouse is worth quoting at length:

> Perhaps the Münster episode led the Protestant Reformers to reaffirm Augustinian amillennialism. Each of the three main Protestant traditions of the sixteenth century—Lutheran, Calvinist, and Anglican—had the support of the state and so continued the same Constantinian approach to theology. Both Luther and Calvin were very suspicious of millennial speculation. Calvin declared that those who engaged in calculations based on the apocalyptic portions of Scripture were "ignorant" and "malicious." The major statements of the various Protestant bodies such as the Augsburg Confession (1, xvii), the Thirty-nine Articles (IV), and the Westminster Confession (chapters 32-33), although professing faith in the return of Christ, do not support apocalyptic millenarian specu-

lation. In certain respects, however, the Reformers inaugurated changes which would lead to a revival of interest in Premillennialism. These include a more literal approach to the interpretation of Scripture, the identification of the papacy with Antichrist, and an emphasis on Bible prophecy.[36]

This explains the amillennialism of the three main Protestant traditions, but not the eschatology of Menno Simons and the Mennonites, the heirs of the Anabaptist-Melchiorite movement.

Menno Simons and Millennialism

Menno Simons resigned the Catholic priesthood and aligned himself with the so-called Anabaptist movement in 1536. This was the same year the authorities executed the surviving leaders of the Münster Kingdom and the same year John Calvin published the first edition of his *Institutes of the Christian Religion*. The Münster fiasco was still fresh in the minds of many. Peter Simons, possibly Menno's own brother, had joined the movement and had died at Oude Klooster (Old Cloister). For Menno the New Jerusalem was a spiritual kingdom which one enters by faith not by violence. It is the cross of Christ that one must take up, not the power of the sword.

The year after he joined the peaceful wing of the Melchiorites, Menno was ordained an elder and began to exercise leadership. The irenic Menno encouraged the dispirited flock to look for a spiritual kingdom. Others who wished to establish an earthly kingdom of God by force of the sword Menno designated "corrupt sects." Münster had besmirched the whole Anabaptist movement. All who advocated believer's baptism were linked with Münster and said to be the same kind of radical Chiliasts who would destroy the whole social fabric if they were given freedom to practice their heresy. Thus Menno complains in his *Foundation of Christian Doctrine*, "At this point I know right well that we have to hear of Münster, kingdom, polygamy, sword, plunder, murder, and the like abominations and scandals which you assert result from baptism." He proceeds to accuse his accusers of using the alleged connection with the "seditious sects and conspiracies" as a justification for their own "blood-shedding."[37]

The idea of an earthly millennium, Menno believed, came from the heretic Cerinthus, who "maintained that the world was created by angels, that Christ was no more than a mere man and had not yet risen, but should rise with us in the future, and thereafter reign one thousand years in the flesh with His saints."[38] Münsterites were in the line of heretics like Cerinthus, not in his camp. Apparently Menno rejected premillennialism as heretical. For Menno, like Augustine, Christ's kingdom was spiritual and eternal, not physical and earthly. Addressing the "corrupt sects" he remonstrates,

> O miserable, erring sheep . . . I have pointed out to
> the magistrates that the kingdom of Christ is not of
> this visible, tangible, transitory world, but that it is an
> eternal, spiritual, and abiding kingdom which is not
> eating and drinking, but righteousness, peace, and joy
> in the Holy Ghost.[39]

Moreover, he charges the "corrupt sects" with having a perverted eschatology. In words that sound like an explicit critique of Joachimite eschatology, Menno declares, "You contend that another dispensation is beginning," which he said was a denial of the Son of God and the Scriptures.[40] Echoing Augustine he insists, "The Scriptures teach that there are two opposing princes and two opposing kingdoms: the one is the Prince of Peace; the other is the prince of strife. Each of these princes had his particular kingdom and as the prince is so is also the kingdom."[41]

The elect do not bring the kingdom with the sword, but Christ Himself brings punishment on evil when He returns and then the eternal dominion begins. "The Scriptures clearly testify that the Lord Christ must first come again before all His enemies are punished," maintains Menno in *The Blasphemy of John of Leiden.* He continues by quoting a series of New Testament Scriptures to affirm that the coming of Christ is visible. He then goes to Daniel to affirm that Christ is given an everlasting dominion.[42] To answer his critics, Menno wrote his *Brief and Clear Confession.* In this concise document he has a simple creedal statement which includes the following:

> This same man, Christ Jesus, preached, was cruci-
> fied, died, and was buried. He rose and ascended to

heaven and is seated at the right hand of the Almighty father, according to the testimony of all Scripture. From thence He will come to judge the sheep and the goats, the good and the evil, the living and the dead. II Cor. 5:10; II Tim. 4:1.

Menno seems not to exceed this in his eschatology. The Mennonite Church, the largest surviving group which traces itself back to Menno and the Anabaptist movement, has historically been amillennial in its eschatology. Its first official confession of faith was adopted in "Dortrecht" [sic], Holland in 1632. The Confession affirms a general resurrection where all will be judged before the judgment seat of Christ. The good will be separated from the evil and "as the blessed of their Father, be received by Christ into eternal life . . . and they shall reign and triumph with Christ forever and ever." References cited include Daniel 12:2, First Corinthians 15 and First Thessalonians 4:13. There is no reference to a millennium.[43] Apparently Menno's seventeenth-century followers were not Chiliasts either.

Calvin and the Millennium

In 1536, the same year Menno left the priesthood to become a member of a persecuted sect, John Calvin published the first edition of his *Institutes of the Christian Religion,* in which he maintained that French Protestants were neither Anabaptists nor anarchists; they intended neither to destroy the French monarchy nor attempt to establish an earthly kingdom of the saints. What they professed was simply the historic Christian faith. Calvin was a disciple of Augustine not the Chiliasts.

Calvin was on his way to Strassburg in 1536 to pursue his studies in peace when he stopped off in Geneva. Guillaume Farel, who was leading the Reformed forces, challenged Calvin to remain or risk God's curse on his studies. Fearing God, Calvin stayed and assisted in the reorganization until he and Farel were put out of the city in 1538. Calvin debated Anabaptists in Geneva in 1537 and again during his brief exile in Strassburg (1538-41). They were probably Melchiorites.[44] Upon his return to Geneva, he further refined his presbyterian system of church government and his Reformed system of theology, usually called Calvinism. Calvin in his *Ecclesiastical Ordinances* promoted the autonomy of the congregation, the independence of Holy Communion and the discipline (the ban) by the church rather than the state. Thus, according to Williams, "Calvinism on the disciplinary side would have appeared closer to Anabaptism than to the magisterial Lutheranism."[45]

John Calvin in his *Institutes of the Christian Religion* has a quick and easy answer to the question of the millennium. For him there is no such thing as an earthly thousand-year reign of Christ in any form. Those who hold to such a doctrine are like those who deny the resurrection of the body. The whole notion is passed off as another work of Satan that has "befuddled men's senses." Paul had to defend the resurrection and overthrow those who denied it (1 Corinthians 15:12 ff.). The subsequent dangerous error was the false doctrine of the millennium held by Chiliasts.

> But a little later there followed the Chiliasts, who limited the reign of Christ to a thousand years. Now their fiction is too childish either to need or to be worth a refutation. And the Apocalypse, from which they undoubtedly drew a pretext for their error, does not support them. For the number "one thousand" [Revelation 20:4] does not apply to the eternal blessedness of the church but only to various disturbances that awaited the church, while still toiling on earth.[46]

Note the expressions, *fiction, childish, pretext* and *error*. Apparently Calvin was not impressed with those who understood John to be expounding a literal thousand-year reign of Christ on earth after His *parousia*. Moreover, Calvin repudiated all the teachings of those commonly branded Anabaptist, finding them not "to be worthy of a refutation."

Worse than this, they fling reproach upon Christ and His kingdom. "Those who assign the children of God to a thousand years in which to enjoy the inheritance of the life to come do not realize how much *reproach* they are casting upon Christ and his Kingdom."[47] In fact, they are guilty of making Christ's kingdom a temporary realm and deny the power and grace of God. "In short, either such persons are *utterly ignorant* of everything divine or they are trying by a *devious malice* to *bring to nought* all the grace of God and power of Christ, the fulfillment of which is realized only when sin is blotted out, death swallowed up, and everlasting life fully restored."[48] Thus this dishonorable teaching is comparable to a repudiation of the resurrection, an essential teaching of

Scripture. Undeniably Calvin set the standard for Reformed theology; stinging phrases, such as *devious malice, utterly ignorant, cast reproach*, help one understand why not a few of his followers easily dismiss premillennialism.

It would be in the seventeenth century that premillennialism entered the magisterial denominations. In 1527 two books were published, *The Beloved City* by the Reformed theologian Johann Heinrich Alsted, and *Clavis Apocalyptica* by the Anglican Joseph Mede.[49] Both advocated premillennialism; nevertheless, premillennialism remained a minority view until the nineteenth century.

Endnotes

1. Principal works drawn upon include the following: John Baille, ed., *Library of Christian Classics*. 26 vols. (London: SCM Press, 1953-69); Norman Cohn, *The Pursuit of the Millennium: Revolutionary Messianism in Medieval and Reformation Europe and its Bearing on Modern Totalitarian Movements*, 2nd ed. (New York: Harper, 1961); F.L. Cross and E.A. Livingstone, eds., *Oxford Dictionary of the Christian Church* (New York: Oxford, 1957 & 1974); Walter A. Elwell, ed., *Evangelical Dictionary of Theology* (Grand Rapids: Baker, 1984); Robert G. Clouse, ed., *The Meaning of the Millennium: Four Views* (Downers Grove: InterVarsity, 1977), hereafter cited as *Meaning*; George H. Williams, *The Radical Reformation* (Philadelphia: Westminster, 1952).

2. Frank N. Magill, *Masterpieces of World Philosophy in Summary Form* (New York: Harper & Row, 1961), 258-263.

3. Robert G. Clouse, "Views of the Millennium," *Evangelical Dictionary of Theology*, 716; hereafter cited as "Views."

4. *City of God*, 20, 7, 518.

5. Ibid.

6. Ibid., 519.

7. Ibid., 20, 8, 521.

8. Ibid., 20, 11, 527.

9. Ibid., 528.

10. Clouse, *Meaning*, 9.

11. "The Sibylline Oracles," *Oxford Dictionary of the Christian Church*, 1252-53.

12. *City of God*, 18, 23, pp. 426-28. "The sibyl of Erythrae certainly wrote some things concerning Christ which are quite manifest. . . ." He notes that the Latin translation is bad, but in the Greek the first letter of each line forms the words, literally "Jesus Christ of-God Son Savior," forms an acrostic for the Greek word *ιχθυς*, fish, commonly used as a symbol for Jesus by the early church.

13. Constantine, by favoring the Church in the fourth century, had set a precedent for messianic emperor figures to come.

14. Cohn, 18.

15. His major works are *Liber Concordiae Novi ac Veteris Testamenti* and *Expositio in Apocalysium* and *Psaltarium Decem Cordarum*. See "Joachim of Fiore," *The Oxford Dictionary of the Christian Church*, 727.

16. Note also the use of "1260" in the Apocalypse (11:3, 12:6). The only other use of the word "one thousand" ($\chi\iota\lambda\iota\omega$) is in Second Peter 3:8, where Peter reminds us that one day and a thousand years are alike to God. Forty-two months are also spoken of in the Apocalypse (11:2, 13:5). If the forty-two months equal 1260 days and if the days are transitioned into years, the system works. Commenting on the reign of the first beast of Revelation 13, A.B. Simpson uses the 1260 as the years of his political power which he surmises begins in 610 with "the decree of [the Eastern Roman Emperor] Phocas establishing the supremacy of the Pope." This brings him to 1870, the year "when the death blow was finally struck at the temporal power of the papacy" (A.B. Simpson, *Heaven Opened: or Exposition of the Book of Revelation* [Nyack, NY: Christian Alliance Publishing Co., 1899], 131-32). Apparently Simpson reckoned that much of Revelation was actually history by his times, possibly the indirect influence of Joachimite eschatology.

17. Cohn, 99-100.

18. Simpson disagrees. "The word 'virgins' is used in the masculine here to denote a life severed and separated from all illicit and unholy things. . . . [T]he Bible nowhere casts a slur on lawful marriage as a less holy state than celibacy" (Simpson, 144). Simpson considers Revelation 14 to be concerned with holiness and missions. "It is very significant that the Holy Spirit has here grouped together two movements which are the peculiar spiritual features of our days. One is the movement for scriptural holiness and the other the great missionary movement to give the gospel as a witness immediately to the nations" (Ibid., 146). The words of John are contemporary. The message of judgment is also important. "Is this not a marked feature of the missionary movement of this Age?" asks Simpson (Ibid., 148).

19. Franciscan Spirituals may have influenced some sixteenth-century Anabaptists.

20. Cohn, 100-101.

21. Mount Tabor had a long history in Israel. On the occasion of the enslavement of Israel by the Canaanites, God called Deborah, the prophetess and judge, to emancipate the Israelites (Judges 4-5). She commissioned Barak to ascend Mount Tabor and gather an army for the deliverance of God's people. Coming down into the valley of Jezreel at the base of Mount Megiddo, he defeated the Canaanites "by the waters of Megiddo" (Judges 5:19). The sole reference to Megiddo in the New Testament is in the Apocalypse. John foresees the gathering of the kings for "the battle of that great day of God Almighty. . . . And he gathered them together into a place called in the Hebrew tongue Armageddon" (Revelation 16:14, 16, KJV). The fifteenth-century Taborites could not miss the connection between old Mount Tabor and the eschatological Battle of Armageddon. Additionally Cohn proposes that the Taborites named the local river Jordan and their city Tabor for the Mount of Olives. "While the former became the Jordan, the latter became the Mount of Olives where Christ had foretold his parousia (Mark XIII), where he had ascended to heaven and where, traditionally, he was expected to reappear in majesty" (Cohn, 230).

22. Ibid., 225.

23. Ibid., 226.

24. Ibid., 252.

25. In Hans J. Hillerbrand, *The Reformation: A Narrative History Related by Contemporary Observers and Participants* (New York: Harper and Rowe, 1964), 224.

26. Williams, 46. "Characteristic of the *Prague Manifesto* is the open espousal of the Storchite-Taborite chiliasm which justifies the violence of the elect" (Ibid., 49).

27. Müntzer does this in his *Von dem gedicheten Glauben* (Ibid., 51).

28. Williams, 54.

29. "The elect friends of God will learn to prophesy. . . . God will do marvelous things with his elect," wrote Müntzer in his "Prague Manifesto" (Hillerbrand, 223-24). Williams observes, "Luther with his argumentation from the written Word and Müntzer with his argumentation out of the compulsion of the Spirit could never have debated from the same platform" (Williams, 57).

30. Cohn, 261.

31. See "Resolution of the Minority," B.J. Kidd, *Documents Illustrative of the Continental Reformation* (Oxford: At the Clarendon Press, 1911), 243-44.

32. Cohn, 279.

33. In his *Exposition of the XII Chapter of Daniel* he predicted the end of the world in 1533 (Williams, 261).

34. Ibid., 288.

35. It seems even some Protestants preferred a Catholic prince-bishop over an Anabaptist peasant kingdom. Luther's prince might turn his territory into a Protestant state; Zwingli might convince the Town Council to change the religion of the canton; Calvin might agree to overthrow the authority of the bishop and establish a Reformed clerocracy; but peasants must endure affliction from both Catholic and Protestant rulers.

36. Clouse, "Views," 716-17.

37. *The Complete Writings of Menno Simons, c. 1496-1561,* tr. and ed. Leonard Verduin (Scottdale, PA: Herald Press, 1956), 197.

38. Ibid., 199.

39. Ibid., 217. The "corrupt sects" included the mob at Münster, the Batenburgers, the Davidians and other Dutch fanatics, usually labeled Anabaptists.

40. Ibid., 219.

41. Ibid., 554.

42. Ibid., 47-48.

43. *Confession of Faith and Minister's Manual,* compiled by J.F. Funk (Scottdale, PA: Mennonite Publishing House, 1942), 31.

44. In Geneva he debated John Bomeromenus of Strassburg and John Stordeur of Liege. In Strassburg he convinced the latter to turn to the Reformed faith. After Stordeur died, Calvin married his widow, Idolette de Bure (Van Buren), who gave Calvin his only child (Williams, 587, 591).

45. Ibid., 596. This may be a factor which later induced many former Dutch Melchiorites to espouse the Reformed faith.

101

46. John Calvin, *Institutes of the Christian Religion*, ed. John T. McNeill, tr. Ford L. Battles (Philadelphia: Westminster, 1960), 3.25.5, II, 995. Calvin made numerous editions of his *Institutes*. All quotations come from the 1559 Latin edition, not the first in 1536, thus reflecting his mature estimation of Anabaptism. Williams (598), however, argues that Calvin grouped divergent opponents as Anabaptists and "did not clearly distinguish between his opponents."

47. Calvin, II, 995.

48. Ibid., II, 996. Italics mine.

49. Clouse, *Meaning*, 10-11, 213 (fn. 4).

Beyond Fantasy:
Tolkien, Lewis and Rowling

Richard Abanes

EDITOR'S NOTE: *Richard Abanes, though not a member of The Christian and Missionary Alliance, is no stranger to Christian Publications, having written a number of books for us. For this reason, and because of the timeliness of the message, we have chosen to include this chapter from his latest book,* Harry Potter and the Bible, *in which he addresses the occult themes in J.K. Rowling's "Harry Potter" series of children's books and compares it to the writings of such classic children's fantasy authors as C.S. Lewis and J.R.R. Tolkien.*

> *"Stop comparing* Harry Potter *to* The Lord of the Rings. . . . Rowling's series is elitist kiddie fare that serves to make modern American children even more narcissistic than they are, and Tolkien's is a masterpiece and—this is crucial—a completely adult tragedy with profound moral and religious implications."*
>
> Mark Gauvreau Judge[1]
> commentator, *Baltimore City Paper*

In an effort to deflect concerns about Rowling's books, Potter supporters have consistently likened the Harry Potter series to the works of J.R.R. Tolkien and C.S. Lewis. This has been done continuously through an unending stream of news stories, interviews and book reviews. The following statement by Judy Corman, spokesperson for Scholastic Press (J.K. Rowling's U.S. publisher), is typical: "There's something these parents are missing, which is it's a magical book. It takes its place along the best in classic literature for children, along with . . . *The Chronicles of Narnia* [C.S. Lewis] and *The Lord of the Rings* [J.R.R. Tolkien]."[2] A similar comment appeared in a Knight-Ridder News Service story: "Rowling's books are not so much anti-Christian as they are fully Christian, drawing on the legacy of fellow British writers C.S. Lewis and J.R.R. Tolkien, whose popular children's tales about the magical lands of Narnia and Middle Earth were written as Christian allegory."[3]

But such a position is seriously flawed, most obviously because the fantasy tales of Tolkien and Lewis fall within the category of mythopoetic literature, meaning that they take place in worlds disassociated from the real world in which we live. As Dr. Curt Brannan of Washington's Bear Creek School District observes: "[In Lewis' and Tolkien's works] there is no confusion in the child's mind . . . that these are mythical characters in a mythical place."[4]

But the Harry Potter books are not mythopoetic. Unlike Lewis' and Tolkien's creations, Rowling's fantasy is set in our twenty-first-century world, complete with contemporary forms of occultism (e.g., astrology and divination) and references to persons and events from our own human history (e.g., Nicholas Flamel, Hand of Glory, Witch Hunts). Rowling's novels also use a vastly different definition of "magic" than the one used by Lewis and Tolkien. Furthermore, the Harry Potter series promotes a concept of right and wrong that is radically altered from the one presented by Lewis and Tolkien.

Remembering Tolkien

English literature professor John Ronald Reuel Tolkien (1892-1973) is commonly viewed as the father of contemporary fantasy. Although he authored a number of brilliant works, his most famous ones are *The Hobbit* and The Lord of the Rings epic trilogy (*The Fellowship of the Ring*, *The Two Towers* and *The Return of the King*). All of these tales interconnect with one another and occur in "Middle-Earth," a complex world Tolkien created with his commanding knowledge of linguistics, history and mythology.

The Hobbit, originally published in 1937, tells the story of Bilbo Baggins, who is a "hobbit." According to Tolkien, hobbits are

> little people, about half our height. . . . There is little or no magic about them, except the ordinary everyday sort which helps them to disappear quietly and quickly when large stupid folk like you and me come blundering along, making a noise like elephants which they can hear a mile off. They are inclined to be fat in the stomach; they dress in bright colours (chiefly green and yellow); wear no shoes, because their feet grow natural leathery soles and thick warm brown hair like the stuff on their heads (which is curly); have long clever brown fingers, good-natured faces, and laugh deep fruity laughs (especially after dinner, which they have twice a day when they can get it).[5]

Bilbo's adventures begin with a visit from a powerful wizard named Gandalf. He reveals that Bilbo's destiny is to travel with a group of thirteen dwarves to a Mountain where Smaug, an evil dragon, dwells. The group's goal will be to slay the dragon and capture his treasure, which rightfully belongs to the dwarves. Throughout this quest they face numerous hardships (e.g., storms, hunger, fatigue, etc.) and dangers (e.g., trolls, goblins, evil wolves and giant spiders). Additionally, when Bilbo becomes separated from the group, he confronts an especially evil creature named Gollum. Eventually, Bilbo escapes Gollum, reunites with the dwarves and Smaug is slain. Bilbo then returns home with a number of treasures, including a magic ring with which he can become invisible and a sword that glows when goblins are near.

Tolkien's The Lord of the Rings trilogy begins sixty years after the conclusion of *The Hobbit*, and finds Bilbo making preparations for his 111th birthday. It will be a special birthday in that Bilbo plans to use the occasion to leave the Shire (where hobbits live) and bequeath all of his possessions, including his house, to his nephew, Frodo. His hope is to do some peaceful traveling and visit the mountains one last time before he dies. And so, at the conclusion of his party, he slips on his magical ring and disappears right before everyone's eyes. Frodo moves into Bilbo's home, and among all of his inherited possessions is the left-behind magic ring, which Gandalf the wizard now suspects is a very dangerous item.

As the trilogy progresses, Gandalf reveals that Bilbo's ring, which now belongs to Frodo, is actually one of three magical rings created in the distant past. In fact, it is the most powerful one, originally owned by the Dark Lord, Sauron, who had tried in ages past to conquer all of Middle-Earth. Sauron was eventually forced into hiding after being vanquished by an army of Elves and Men, but in *The Fellowship of the Ring*, he has risen again and is seeking the ring in order to fully restore his former powers. The only way dwellers of Middle-Earth will ever defeat Sauron is if Frodo destroys the ring by throwing it into the volcanic fires of the Crack of Doom in which it was forged, in the depths of Orodruin, beneath the Fire Mountain.

The remainder of the trilogy follows Frodo and his three hobbit companions (Sam, Merry and Pippin) on their mission to destroy the ring. Along the way, they are separated, forced to flee evil "Black Riders" (deadly phantoms); fight Orcs and evil wolves; evade a traitorous wizard named Saruman; and battle internal psychological stresses caused by the ring.

By the time Frodo reaches the Crack of Doom, Sauron's evil Hordes have converged on the last stronghold of the forces of good, and a final Armageddon-like battle ensues. Fortunately, the ring is destroyed just when all hope seems lost. Sauron's power is broken once and for all, the forces of good triumph and Middle- Earth is saved from the Dark Lord's tyranny. But it is a bitter-sweet victory. Although Sauron has been defeated, the destruction of the ring marks the beginning of the end of Middle- Earth, the allotted time for which has passed. The world of Hobbits, Dwarves and Elves must give way to the time of Men.

This brief summary of *The Hobbit* and The Lord of the Rings trilogy cannot begin to do justice to the masterful tale Tolkien weaves using his expansive imagination and brilliant mind. He was truly one of the most gifted writers of the last 200 years, easily on the level of Dickens, Jane Austen or Mark Twain.[6] *The Hobbit* and The Lord of the Rings trilogy, because of their superior literary quality, unique storylines and timeless nature, certainly deserve a place among the classics.

Now compare Tolkien's work with the Harry Potter books. According to a number of insightful reviewers, the Potter books are little more than occult-glamorizing, morally bleak, marketing sensations filled with one-dimensional characters and a hero who is, to borrow the words of Rowling's Professor Snape, "a nasty little boy who considers rules to be beneath him."[7]

For example, British commentator Anthony Holden, judged her books to be "not particularly well-written."[8] Roger Sutton, editor of *The Horn Book* (a seventy-five-year-old children's literary digest in Boston), has described the Potter books as a "critically insignificant" series, adding that as literature, they are "nothing to get excited about."[9] And in his article for ScienceFictionFantasy.net, Sherwood Smith observed: "The adults are conveniently stupid when needed to keep the kids in the action, refusing to listen just when any other adult would see alarms. The headmaster, supposedly benevolent and omniscient, seems content to permit the beginners to face death over and over, sure they will somehow win. But of course they do."[10] An even more caustic review has come from renowned literary critic Harold Bloom, who made scathing remarks about Rowling's works on the PBS interview program, *Charlie Rose*: "[T]here's nothing there to read," Bloom asserted. "They're just an endless string of clichés. I cannot think that does anyone any good. That's not *Wind in the Willows*. That's not *Through the Looking Glass*. . . . It's really just slop."[11]

It seems apparent that J.K. Rowling is no J.R.R. Tolkien. But if there is such a disparity between Rowling's novels and Tolkien's classics, why are they still being compared to each other? It may stem from the fact that both include: 1) a struggle between good and evil; 2) use of the word "magic"; and 3) "wizard" characters. These superficial similarities, however, do not justify putting both writers in the same league. In fact, upon close examination, the "similarities" do not really exist.

First, the struggle between good and evil in *The Hobbit* and The Lord of the Rings trilogy relies heavily on, and is rooted in, Tolkien's devout Christian faith. His good characters are truly good. His evil characters are truly evil. And when any good character commits an evil deed, he suffers as a result of his actions, or at the very least, he must do something to atone for his behavior. Tolkien's stories also do not include episodes of good characters doing bad things (e.g., lying to friends or stealing from authority figures) in order to accomplish a good task.

Furthermore, Tolkien's moral boundaries are clearly drawn with "good" and "evil" characters behaving in a manner that corresponds to their identities in Middle Earth: Orcs, Trolls and Sauron are evil; Gandalf, Hobbits, Elves and Dwarves are generally good. In Rowling's novels, however, moral ambiguity and relativism abound, while at the same time no one really seems to know exactly who is and who is not evil. In the Harry Potter series, one's best friend might turn out to be an enemy, while an enemy might actually be one's closest ally.

Second, the "magic" most often seen in Tolkien's novels is not the kind of occult-based/contemporary-pagan magick Rowling employs. In fact, Tolkien disliked the word "magic," but was forced to use it because he could find no other word closer to the meaning he intended. He attempted to fix this problem in Middle- Earth by including strict limitations on magic, its nature, who has it, how it is used and why it is used. Even so, Tolkien often complained that the word "magic" failed to adequately, or accurately, explain his meaning.

Various letters written by Tolkien make it clear that his definition of "magic" in the context of Middle-Earth does not include any kind of supernatural power. It is a natural ability given *only* to Elves. No other race—including Orcs, Trolls, Dwarves, Hobbits and others—has magical capabilities. In Letter #155, published in *The Letters of J.R.R. Tolkien*, Tolkien writes: "[A] difference in the use of 'magic' in this story is that it is not to come by [i.e., acquired] by 'lore' or spells; but is in an inherent power not possessed by Men as such."[12]

For Elves, however, "magic" is as natural as singing or drawing. In fact, Tolkien actually described it simply as "Art" without human limitations.[13] The source of it rests within Elves themselves. It depends on no external power, nor can it be learned or enhanced. The very term "magic" is perplexing to Elves when they hear it being used by mortals to describe their abilities. This is apparent in *The Fellowship of the Ring*, when Galadriel (Elven "Lady of Lorien") shows Frodo her "magic" mirror, saying: "For this is what your folk would call magic, I believe; though I do not understand clearly what they mean. . . . But this, if you will, is the magic of Galadriel."[14]

The other kind of magic that exists in Middle-Earth is magic within various objects (e.g., weapons, rings, helmets, mirrors, etc.). But these items, too, hold a different type of magic than the objects in Rowling's works (e.g., Mr. Weasley's Flying Car, Harry's Marauder's Map and his invisibility cape). The items on the Harry Potter series are bewitched or enchanted. However, the objects in Tolkien's fantasy receive special qualities through "lore," which Tolkien likened to technology and science. They are created in accordance with the laws of nature as found in Middle-Earth.[15]

Interestingly, drastic and negative consequences always result in Middle-Earth when its non-magical dwellers (non-Elves) get too close to magic. For example, nine Men, each of whom are given magical rings by the dark wizard Sauron, eventually turn into evil phantoms (i.e., ringwraiths) enslaved by Sauron. The one ring Bilbo possesses begins to corrupt him, just as it had corrupted its previous owners. Frodo, after his long journey with Bilbo's magical ring, is never physically or psychologically the same. He tells Gandalf he has been forever "wounded" by the ordeal.[16] And every year on the anniversary of the ring's destruction, he becomes bedridden with nausea.[17] Obviously, the properties of "magic" are very different in Middle-Earth.

But what about Tolkien's many "wizards" (e.g., Gandalf and Sauron)? Do these characters not mirror the kind of wizards that are in Harry Potter? In a word, no. Any argument to the contrary exposes a superficial understanding of the nature of magic in Tolkien's novels. Alan Jacobs of Wheaton College, for instance, although a well-respected literature professor, has on numerous occasions put forth this groundless argument:

> I was eagerly describing Harry Potter to a good friend of mine . . . [A]nd he said, "You know, I'm a little nervous about this. I mean, you know, witches, wizardry, magic. I don't know whether I want to read a book like this to my kids." And I said, "Well, doesn't your family enjoy *The Lord of the Rings*?" And he said, "We revere *The Lord of the Rings*." . . . And I said, "But, isn't there a lot of magic, and isn't Gandalf a wizard?" And he said, "Yeah, I guess that's right."[18]

Jacobs' analogy is faulty because Rowling's wizards are human, whereas Tolkien's "wizards" are not human at all. Gandalf is a "Maia"—i.e., an angelic-like being that has taken on human form. Sauron, the evil wizard in The Lord of the Rings trilogy, is also a Maia, albeit a fallen one. According to Tolkien, the Maiar (plural for Maia) were sent into Middle-Earth by the Valar (an even higher order of angelic beings) to render assistance to Elves and Men.[19]

Gandalf and Sauron, along with every other wizard in Middle- Earth (e.g., the evil Saruman, another Maia) are, in essence, illustrations of good angels and evil angels (or demons). Hence, their powers are part of their nature and not obtained through occultism. This also would hold true for the evil Melkor—perhaps the most powerful of all the Valar—who tried to subjugate Middle-Earth in direct rebellion against the creator of all things, Eru, also known as the One or Ilúvatar (i.e., God).

In Tolkien's writings Elves, the Maiar and Valar are simply exercising their God-given abilities when they do "magic," either for good or for evil. In J.K. Rowling's world, however, wizards are human and their magickal powers are tapped/increased through occultism. Furthermore, *there is no Ilúvatar (i.e., God) overseeing the battle between good and evil.* This is by far the most profound difference between Rowling's books and the works of Tolkien.

Beyond a limited number of vague similarities, Tolkien's works and those of J.K. Rowling are vastly different. The chasm that separates their fantasies was concisely expressed by Mark Gauvreau Judge in a June 12, 2000 *Baltimore City Paper* article titled "The Trouble With Harry":

> [T]he power of *The Lord of the Rings* is the heavy undercurrent of tragedy and loss that runs through the story. Tolkien's masterwork is about growing up, the loss of enchantment, and the Christian paradox of salvation through suffering and painful death. . . . These themes are expressed in the trilogy's central conundrum: If Hobbit Frodo, thrust by circumstance into the role of Ring-Bearer, fails in his mission, evil overwhelms the world. If he succeeds, he unravels his own world. As the angelic Elf Queen Galadriel tells him, "Do you not see wherefore your coming to us is the footstep of doom? For if you fail, then we are laid bare to the Enemy. Yet if you succeed, then our power is diminished, and [our kingdom] will fade, and the time and tides will sweep it away."
>
> In other words, like mortal life, this Ring business is a no-win situation. Indeed, the heroic Ring-Bearer never recovers from his mission. . . . Frodo sacrifices everything for the world because he answered to the higher calling of conscience and duty, even if that meant enduring the slings and arrows of the world's Muggles. Would Harry and his pals do the same?[20]

Would Harry and his pals do the same thing? Probably not. In *Harry Potter and the Sorcerer's Stone*, we learn how wizards/ witches feel about helping others (specifically, Muggles) with their magic. On page 65 of Book I, Harry asks Hagrid why wizards do not tell Muggles about their existence. In his reply, Hagrid explains that Muggles would just keep bothering wizards/witches for assistance with their problems, then he concludes: "Nah, we're best left alone."[21]

This is a far cry from the kind of response Frodo gives after Gandalf tells him he has two choices set before him: 1) take on the terrible burden of destroying the ring to help save others from Sauron, and in so doing, leave his beloved home at Bag End, in the Shire; or 2) give the responsibility to someone else. Frodo exhibits a very un-Harry-Potter-like sense of duty, sacrificing his own life and concerns for those of his neighbors:

> "As far as I understand what you have said, I sup-pose I must keep the Ring and guard it, at least for the present, whatever it may do to me. . . . [I]n the mean-while it seems that I am a danger, a danger to all that live near me. I cannot keep the Ring and stay here. I ought to leave Bag End, leave the Shire, leave every-thing and go away." He sighed. "I should like to save the Shire, if I could—though there have been times when I thought the inhabitants too stupid and dull for words, and have felt that an earthquake or an invasion of dragons might be good for them. But I don't feel like that now. I feel that as long as the Shire lies be-hind, safe and comfortable, I shall find wandering more bearable: I shall know that somewhere there is a firm foothold, even if my feet cannot stand there again. Of course, I have sometimes thought of going away, but I imagined that as a kind of holiday, a series of adventures like Bilbo's or better, ending in peace. But this would mean exile, a flight from danger into danger, drawing it after me. And I suppose I must go alone, if I am to do that and save the Shire. But I feel very small, and very uprooted, and well—desperate. The Enemy is so strong and terrible."[22]

The most critical difference between Rowling and Tolkien is the spiritual perspectives from which they created their stories. Tolkien was unabashedly Christian. In one of his letters, he wrote: "With regard to The Lord of the Rings . . . I actually intended it to be consonant with Christian thought and belief, which is asserted elsewhere."[23] In Letter #310, he openly declared:

So it may be said that the chief purpose of life, for any one of us, is to increase according to our capacity our knowledge of God by all the means we have, and to be moved by it to praise and thanks. To do as we say in the Gloria in Excelsis . . . "We praise you, we call you holy, we worship you, we proclaim your glory, we thank you for the greatness of your splendour."[24]

To date, Rowling's only public statements of any spiritual significance is a brief and rather flippant remark made during a 1999 interview, in response to a question about her personal beliefs: "Well, as it happens, I believe in God, but there's no pleasing some people!"[25]

A Look at Lewis

English scholar Clive Staples Lewis (1898-1963), who was a close friend of Tolkien, authored numerous books explaining and defending Christianity: *The Screwtape Letters* (1942), *Miracles* (1947) and *Mere Christianity* (1952), to name but a few. He also excelled at writing both fantasy and science fiction. Perhaps his most famous work is The Chronicles of Narnia series of seven volumes, which for the most part, detail the adventures of four children surnamed Pevensie: Peter, Susan, Edmund and Lucy.[26]

The stories take place in Narnia, a land reached by way of a secret multidimensional doorway located, of all places, at the back of a common wardrobe. Lucy is the first to discover the hidden passageway, but she is soon followed by her sister and brothers. All of them eventually become entangled in a great Narnian conflict between forces of good and evil. This war places the armies of a wicked White Witch against the followers of the Great Lion, Aslan, the son of the Emperor Beyond the Sea.

It all began when the White Witch seized control of Narnia and turned the once beautiful land into a dreary world where it is always winter, but never Christmas. Eventually, the Witch is defeated, Aslan's loyal subjects are freed, spring returns to Narnia and the four children are crowned as kings and queens. The four children return to our world, but throughout successive books revisit Narnia to live out more adventures with Aslan.

In a news article covering the controversy over using the Harry Potter books in public schools, Children's Librarian Stephanie Bange expressed the following sentiment: "[N]obody makes a fuss about C.S. Lewis' The Chronicles of Narnia series, which are based on Christian theology, but there are also witches and the dark side."[27] Although this type of analogy seems logical and applicable on the surface, closer examination reveals that it is flawed in three ways.

First, the "Christian theology" in Lewis' fantasy is veiled beneath various characters (e.g., Aslan the Lion). Consequently, there is no *direct* association that can be made between the books and any contemporary religion. In Harry Potter, however, a *direct* link to paganism/witchcraft is made via the presentation to readers of current occult beliefs and practices.

Second, there is indeed a witch in the *Narnia* series, but she is evil and based on age-old and widely accepted symbols and illustrations of evil. In contrast, the witches and wizards in Harry Potter are children who have numerous characteristics in common with young readers, including age, attitudes, thoughts, feelings and experiences. Consequently, Rowling's line between fantasy and reality is extremely thin, as evidenced by her own admission that many children believe Hogwarts is a real place (see Rowling quote in Chapter 8).

Third, Lewis does not present a conflict between good and evil based on any "dark side" concepts of power. This "dark side" versus "light side" battle, popularized by "the force" concept in George Lucas' *Star Wars*, is built around the existence of a neutral "power" that has a dark and light side. Conflict arises when persons drawn to the force's dark side ("evil") seek dominion over those who remain faithful to the light side ("good"). Both sides, although they may certainly have different goals, are drawing upon the same "power." The outcome of their battle depends solely on how adept each participant has become at controlling "the force" (i.e., magic). Although a similar "dark side"/"light side" battle exists in the Harry Potter series, it cannot be found in Lewis' novels.

In The Chronicles of Narnia series, the conflict involves two opposing forces (i.e., kinds of magic) of entirely different origins. The one source of magic (Aslan's deep magic) is "good" because it comes from, is controlled by and operates through the One who has legitimate authority over all things (i.e., the Emperor Beyond the Sea). The other source of magic is "evil" because it springs from an illegitimate authority that has usurped control over Narnia (i.e., the White Witch). This clearly distinguishes Lewis' fantasy books from those authored by Rowling.

Closely tied to this issue is the method by which evil is conquered in Lewis' story as opposed to how it is overcome in Rowling's books. Lewis' good characters (e.g., Peter, Lucy, Susan) do not overcome witchcraft by learning more witchcraft. Instead, they respond to evil by becoming servants of the good character, Aslan, who ultimately vanquishes the White Witch. Rowling's good characters, however, seek to overcome evil by using the same dualistic magical power employed by Lord Voldemort and his Death Eaters. In fact, every good witch and wizard has been trained by the same kind of institution that instructed Voldemort and his followers.

Additionally, it must be mentioned that Rowling's works, unlike those of C.S. Lewis, are completely dependent on magick. It is central to her story, whereas Lewis uses magic sparingly and in a highly stylized manner that does not connect with the real world. But the magickal arts used by Harry and his friends are available to children in the occult section of any nearby bookstore or at any number of Internet web sites. As one newspaper columnist observed, "Lewisian magic seems a bit pale and remote compared with Rowling's; it is far easier to imagine a Harry Potter fan thinking: 'Wow, that sounds like fun! If only I could find a way to . . .' "[28]

Another difference between Lewis' books and those produced by Rowling lies in the ultimate meaning of the works. As journalist Alan Cochrum noted in his *Fort-Worth Star Telegram* article, Rowling's novels seem to have no grander purpose than to "provide a rollicking good time."[29] Consequently, her stories are filled with crude jokes, crass remarks, gratuitous violence, gore, juvenile antics and just about every other ploy used in today's action- packed PG-13 films and video games. Lewis' novels, however, offer an immeasurably deeper gift to readers, as Cochrum notes:

> Lewis' books have a very different goal; the British scholar does hope that his readers come away with a good time, and much more as well. His question is: "What would the story of the Bible (Creation, Incarnation, Death-and-Resurrection, Redemption, Revela-

tion) look like in another world?" The answer, in a word, is Aslan—the leonine Christ figure of Narnia.[30]

It also must be recognized that in the works of Lewis and Tolkien issues of "morality and integrity are at stake and dealt with as important and significant concerns."[31] Tolkien, for instance, illustrates right and wrong, good and evil not only through the choices his characters make, but how those choices affect others. His stories raise issues involving the consequences of disobedience, the merits of self-sacrifice, the detrimental effects of negative emotions (e.g., pride, greed, lust, unforgiveness, etc.) and the need to fulfill one's responsibilities for the benefit of others, even when those responsibilities are difficult and painful.

Lewis' tales offer similar morality lessons. The most obvious example involves the disobedience of Edmund Pevensie, a little boy whose errant ways subject him to the power of the wicked White Witch. To rescue Edmund, Aslan offers himself as a sacrifice on the ancient Stone Table. Although he is killed, Aslan rises again through a "deeper" magic unknown to the witch. This sacrificial love convicts Edmund of his evil ways, and he repents of his sins. Ultimately, the once mischievous Edmund is transformed by Aslan's love into Narnia's "King Edmund the Just."

In the Harry Potter series, however, morality is presented inconsistently. Though there are examples of true, admirable courage and loyalty, in too many instances the ethics are muddied. Bad characters turn out to be good. Good characters turn out to be bad. Misbehavior is condoned as long as the eventual outcome is either fun or rewarding (e.g., Harry's lying and disobedience). Good deeds bring about evil results (Harry shows mercy by sparing Pettigrew's life, but this eventually leads to the rising of Voldemort and the murder of Cedric). Harmful deeds are committed to bring about positive results (e.g., Sirius Black, while in the form of a dog, drags Ron into a secret corridor beneath a tree, breaking Ron's leg in the process, in order to get Harry to follow and learn the truth about Peter Pettigrew). In short, Rowling's moral universe is a topsy-turvy world with no firm rules of right and wrong or any godly principles by which to determine the truly good from the truly evil.

Endnotes

1. Mark Gauvreau Judge, "The Trouble With Harry," *Baltimore City Paper*, July 12-18, 2000, available online at www.citypaper.com/2000-07-12/feature2.html.

2. Reuters, "Muggles Seek to Muzzle Harry Potter In Schools," October 13, 1999, available online at www.cesnur.org/recens/potter_04.htm#Anchor-42728.

3. Richard Scheinin, "Harry Potter's Wizardly Powers Divide Opinion," Knight-Ridder News Service, December 3, 1999, available online at http://arlington.net/news/doc/1047/1:FAITH2/1:FAITH2120399.html.

4. Curt Brannan, "What About Harry Potter," available online at www.tbcs.org/.

5. J.R.R. Tolkien, *The Hobbit* (New York: Ballantine Books, 1937; 1982 revised edition), 2.

6. Dozens of books have been written about Tolkien the man, his work and his message. The titles of these study volumes, many of which deal with the unbelievably complex and detailed descriptions of Middle-Earth and its "history," hint at the literary genius they discuss: *J.R.R. Tolkien: Man of Fantasy*; *J.R.R. Tolkien: Myth Maker*; *Between Faith and Fiction: Tolkien and the Powers of His World*; *Tolkien's Legendarium: Essays on the History of Middle-Earth*; and *Recovery and Transcendence for the Contemporary Mythmaker: The Spiritual Dimension in the Works of J.R.R. Tolkien*.

7. J.K. Rowling, *Harry Potter and the Goblet of Fire* (New York: Scholastic Press, 2000), 516.

8. Anthony Holden, quoted in Sarah Lyall, "Wizard vs. Dragon: A Close Contrast, but the Fire-Breather Wins," *New York Times*, January 29, 2000, available online at www.nytimes.com.

9. Roger Sutton, quoted in Elizabeth Mehren, "Wild About Harry," *Los Angeles Times*, July 28, 2000, available online at www.latimes.com.

10. Sherwood Smith, "The Harry Potter Phenomenon," *Science Fiction Fantasy*, available online at www.sff.net.

11. Harold Bloom, quoted in Jamie Allen, "Harry and Hype," July 13, 2000, CNN Online, available online at www.cnn.com/2000/books/news/07/13/potter.hype/.

12. Humphrey Carpenter, *The Letters of J.R.R. Tolkien* (New York: Houghton Mifflin, 1981; 2000 edition), Letter, 155.

13. Carpenter, Letter #131.

14. J.R.R. Tolkien, *The Fellowship of the Ring* (New York: Ballantine Books, 1955; 1982 edition), 427.

15. Carpenter, Letter #153.

16. J.R.R. Tolkien, *The Return of the King* (New York: Ballantine, 1955; 1982 edition), 299.

17. Tolkien, *The Return of the King*, 341.

18. Alan Jacobs, interview on *Mars Hill Audio* (vol. 40, September/October 1999), audio cassette, side 2.

19. See the Tolkien Archives available online at www.tolkien-archives.com/racehistories.shtml.

20. Judge, available online at www.citypaper.com.

21. J.K. Rowling, *Harry Potter and the Sorcerer's Stone* (New York: Scholastic, 1997), 65.

22. Tolkien, *The Fellowship*, 88-89.

23. Carpenter, Letter #269.

24. Carpenter, Letter #310.

25. J.K. Rowling, interview with America Online, May 4, 2000, available at http://www.geocities.com/harrypotterfans/jkraolchat.html.

26. This plot is primarily the storyline in Book II of Lewis' series, although the remaining volumes (III-VII) continue following the adventures of the four children. Book I, however, is somewhat of a precursor to the rest of the volumes, and deals with two other children—Digory Kirke and Polly Plummer—and their struggles against the White Witch, who is known as Jadis in Book I. (Editor's note: The publisher of the Lewis books has in recent years renumbered the books in the series; the endnote above refers to the new numbering scheme.)

27. Stephanie Bange, quoted in Mary McCarty, "Potter's Pouters Puzzling," *Dayton Daily News*, November 3, 1999.

28. Alan Cochrum, "Harry Potter and the Magic Brew-haha," *Fort-Worth Star Telegram*, December 18, 1999, available online at www.fwst.com.

29. Cochrum.

30. Cochrum.

31. Brannan, available online at http://www.tbcs.org/vision/article04.htm.

117

Providences and Providences

K. Neill Foster

It was June, 1988. I had just graduated from seminary a second time (second seminary!). It was Sunday morning, and we were on our way to Canada for the wedding of my nephew, Kevin. Heading north along Interstate 5 in California, as we approached the San Francisco exit, our 1981 Oldsmobile (that we had bought because of its "mint" condition) suddenly began to show itself ordinary after all. In fact, noises—very loud noises—began to emerge from under the hood. I tried to limp along at least into Oakland so that we could hear our son-in-law preach.

It was not to be. My wife finally won the debate about whether we should turn off or not, and I eased into a small town called Dublin. I had not really noticed it on previous trips, but fortunately there were a number of repair shops, and it was also well populated with car agencies.

We pulled into the first station. The mechanic knew immediately what was wrong. It was not good news. It would take several days to fix the problem (we didn't have several days to spare), and it would cost plenty. The decision was made. We would buy a new car. There simply was no time to do anything else.

As we began our Sunday morning itineration around the car lots, I asked the first salesman if there was any establishment we should avoid. He advised that the Nissan agency was in financial trouble and that we had best not go there.

So we started the rounds. It was a long and frustrating day filled with disappointment, ambivalence and pangs of conscience because of the day on which it was being undertaken.

About 4 o'clock, we decided to drop in at the Nissan agency. Never thinking that I could afford a new Maxima, I began looking at the secondhand ones. By this time, the salesman had arrived. He asked me if I would be interested in buying a new Maxima if he could get the price down to where I could handle it.

"Sure," I responded.

He led me over to the spot where two new Maximas were parked. Seemingly within seconds, the sticker price dropped dramatically. The one we liked best was "loaded." I knew as the price plummeted that he was getting close to what we might be able to manage.

By this time my daughter and son-in-law had arrived, so we men made our way to the small cubicle that all car dealerships seem to have. This one was surrounded by glass on three sides. As we sat there dickering, suddenly there was an earthquake—5.0 on the Richter scale, centered at San Jose, a few miles away.

By this time the salesman knew I was a preacher. So as the cubicle creaked and groaned, he said, "There's your sign. Buy the car." I declined. I had also informed the dealership that there was something drastically wrong with my wounded Oldsmobile. They plainly did not want to know the details and brushed my information aside.

Nevertheless, the decision was to "sleep on it." I am sure the salesman thought he would never see us again. My wife claims that he was almost crying as we drove away. That night in Oakland, I remember looking out the window from the third floor apartment and thinking to myself, "If the earthquake hits again, we'll end up over there." There were no more tremors that I knew about.

The next morning when we rose, both of us knew that we were going to buy the car. We had not discussed it; we just had come to a mutual conclusion without talking. It was one of those nonverbal things.

So I filled out a check for a round number, nearly $400 less than the final price of the day before. With check in hand, we returned to the Nissan dealership.

"Here it is. Take it or leave it," I said, having learned that little trick from my dad. That last several hundred dollars must have pushed them over a precipice of some kind. They plainly were not happy. Finally, reluctantly and somewhat disgustedly, they agreed.

I then proceeded to tell them that there was no money in the account on which I had written the check and that they would have to wait till Wednesday to cash the check. Again, they agreed. That Monday afternoon, we unloaded our 1981 Oldsmobile and surrendered it to the graces of the dealership. We put our baggage in the new white Maxima and headed for the Canadian border. All the dealer had left was a check that was useless until Wednesday.

Those who have heard me tell this story have observed that driving away in a new car with a still useless check in the hands of the car dealer is the most dramatic part of the story. The check did clear in due time—and we had a brand new car, plus an amazing story to tell.

But there were things that bothered me. Why did it have to happen on Sunday? Was it really God's providence? I have a Presbyterian streak in me that wants no commerce on the Sabbath! I also knew the biblical account of Jonah. When he started running away from God, a ship was waiting for him—in the wrong place at the wrong time. I couldn't decide whether this "Sunday Maxima" was a gift from God or a ship going to Tarshish.

My wife knew the vacillation of soul I was feeling.

"Quit fussing," she said, "and accept it as a graduation present from God." Weeks later a pastor friend pondered my quandary and said, "I believe it was a gift from the Lord. Accept it that way."

I was at peace. But my wife keeps wondering why our lives just can't be ordinary. I'm not sure I can answer that, but knowing there are providences and providences makes one careful and cautious, as it should.

Biblical and Historical Examples

The word "providence" refers to a set of circumstances that are so highly unusual that they suggest the direct intervention of God in human affairs so as to secure a surprising or unexpected result. Examples abound, both biblical and historical.

- The life of Job began to unravel when Satan sent a wind sounding very much like an earthquake (Job 1:19).

- Elijah, too, was witness to an earthquake, "but the Lord was not in the earthquake" (1 Kings 19:11, Amp.).

- When Jesus rebuked the waves, the suggestion from the Greek *seismos* in the text is that behind the storm was an earthquake that needed rebuke (Matthew 8:23-27; Mark 4:36-41),[1] an earthquake with origins in the nether world.

- When Jesus died, there was an earthquake (Matthew 27:51). There was another earthquake that shook the prison that kept Paul and

Silas. It clearly was from God Almighty and was used to trigger the release of the apostles (Acts 16:25).

- Historically, the Azusa Street movement of 1906 comes to mind. Events in the revival coincided with and were punctuated by the San Francisco earthquake.[2] It was as if the Almighty said, "These events are the mighty work of my Holy Spirit," or at least that would be the impression since providences are often taken to be evidences of the expressed will of God. For some, the San Francisco earthquake which rattled all up and down the west coast was an emphatic and divine witness to the authenticity of the Azusa events.

- Similarly, in recent years, John Wimber welcomed a prophet by the name of Paul Cain to the West Coast. When he arrived, his coming was also punctuated by an earthquake.

In November 1988 Paul Cain gave a prophecy to Jack Deere for Wimber, saying that there would be an earthquake in Southern California the day he [Cain] would arrive to meet Wimber for the first time. This would be a smaller one and a large one would take place elsewhere in the world the day after he left Anaheim. The first earthquake took place near Anaheim on the day he predicted. He left Anaheim on December 7. The large Soviet-Armenian earthquake occurred on December 8.[3]

Obviously Paul Cain was a man of God whose very arrival in Los Angeles was confirmed by nature itself. Or was he? Apparently not. Wimber finally separated himself and the Vineyard from Prophet Cain as errant and strange. But note, even if Cain was indeed a false prophet, as Wimber may have believed, his arrival had nevertheless been punctuated by an earthquake as he predicted. My point is that there are providences and providences. Discerning between them is not always easy, as is evident in this next illustration.

In John Wimber's own ministry there was an event in which tongues were manifested in his assembly. The manifestation left him deeply troubled. Was this of God, or was it not? Carole Wimber tells the story.

> On Mother's Day of 1981 we had a watershed experience that launched us into what today is called power evangelism. At this time John invited a young man who had been attending our church to preach on a Sunday evening. By now we had grown to over 700

participants. The young man shared his testimony, which was beautiful and stirring, then asked for all the people under the age of twenty-five to come forward. None of us had a clue as to what was going to happen. When they got to the front, the speaker said, "For years now the Holy Spirit has been grieved by the Church but He's getting over it. Come Holy Spirit."

And He came.

Most of these young people had grown up around our home—we had four children between the ages of fifteen and twenty-one. We knew the young people well. One fellow, Tim, started bouncing. His arms flung out and he fell over, but one of his hands accidentally hit a mike stand and he took it down with him. He was tangled up in the cord, with the mike next to his mouth. Then he began speaking in tongues, so the sound went throughout the gymnasium [where they were meeting]. We had never considered ourselves charismatics, and certainly had never placed emphasis on tongues. We had seen a few people tremble and fall over before, and we had seen many healings. But this was different. The majority of the young people [over 400] were shaking and falling over. At one point it looked like a battlefield scene, bodies everywhere, people weeping and wailing, speaking in tongues. And Tim in the middle of it all babbling into the microphone. There was much shouting and loud behavior!

John sat quietly, playing the piano and wide-eyed. Members of our staff were fearful and angry. Several people got up and walked out, never to be seen again—at least they were not seen by us.

But I knew God was visiting us. I was so thrilled because I had been praying for power for so long. This might not have been the way I wanted to see it come, but this was how God gave it to us. . . . I asked one boy, who was on the floor, "What's happening to you right now?" He said, "It's like electricity. I can't move." I was amazed by the effect of God's power on the human body. I suppose I thought that it would all be an inward work, such as conviction or repentance. I never imagined there would be strong physical manifestations.

But John wasn't as happy as I. He had never seen large numbers of people sprawled out over the floor. . . . He spent that night reading Scripture and historical accounts of revival from the lives of people like Whitfield and Wesley. . . . But his study did not yield conclusive answers to questions raised from the previous evening's events. By 5 a.m. John was desperate. He cried out to God, "Lord, if this is You, please tell me." A moment later the phone rang and a pastor friend of ours from Denver, Colorado was on the line. "John," he said, "I'm sorry I'm calling so early, but I have something really strange to tell you. I don't know what it means, but God wants me to say, 'It's Me, John.' "[4]

That day, John Wimber, by his wife's testimony, crossed a rubicon: He accepted the providence as from God. Whether it had divine origin or not may still be disputed by some, I suppose, but the Vineyard movement emerged out of Wimber's acceptance of that providence. For some, the existence of the Vineyard is proof enough that the providence was from God. For my part, questioner that I sometimes am, an "it's me" response would not have been enough. I would have wanted to ask, "And who are you?"

Many times, on a lesser scale than the Richter, similar events take place. Good people observe unusual events in a spiritual context and suppose that those providences are the obvious proof of theological orthodoxy and right doctrine. But is that an accurate conclusion? Biblically speaking, the answer must be "no." The Scriptures say, "The coming of the lawless one will be in accordance with the work of Satan displayed in all kinds of counterfeit miracles, signs and wonders, and in every sort of evil that deceives those who are perishing" (2 Thessalonians 2:9-10).

The true criteria by which any providence must be judged are those enduring principles relating to morality, uprightness, character and the final fruit which heaven will reveal. The question is not: Are there miracles and providences? Rather, the question is: Does this minister travel with his own wife and does he pay his bills? Do godly lives and relentless holiness back up the supernatural claims?

Contemporary Events

One of the phenomena of contemporary literature is *The Celestine Prophecy*.[5] An examination of its content reveals the author's fascination with the serendipities of life, with what we are calling here providences or special encounters. Most everyone has them, and the tendency is to give life significance to them. Author Redfield does that in his Celestine series. There is no hint of *divine* providence in his novel, only the fascination with unexpected and unpredicted events of various kinds. It never seems to occur to anyone that such encounters might be good or evil—possibly from God or possibly from Satan—and if from the counterkingdom, a source of deception and delusion.

During the process of writing this book, I received a manuscript that basically embraced and advocated the Toronto Blessing.[6] The author argued passionately and at great length for the providences which "led" him to go to the Toronto event for the first time. The point I am making here is simply that in the cases of the *Celestine Prophecy* and the Toronto Blessing, the arguments are similar, even identical—the first claims *profound* (unassigned) significance to unusual events; the second claims *divine* (assigned) significance to unusual events. The question apparently was never asked: Are these providences from Almighty God or from another source?

Endnotes

1. J.R. Goff, Jr., "Charles Fox Parham," *Dictionary of Pentecostal and Charismatic Movements* (Grand Rapids, MI: Zondervan, 1988), 660-661.

2. G. Bornkamm, VII, *"Seismos," Theological Dictionary of the New Testament* (Grand Rapids MI: Eerdmans, 1985), 1014-1015.

3. Terri Sillivant, "Paul Cain's Ministry: Recent Manifestations of the Spirit" (Grace City Report: Special Edition, n.d.), 6, 15. Varied perspectives on these events exist.

4. John Wimber and Kevin Springer, *Riding the Third Wave* (Basingtoke, Hants, UK: Marshall Pickering, 1987), 45-46.

5. James Redfield, *The Celestine Prophecy* (New York: Warner Books, 1993).

6. An unpublished manuscript submitted to Christian Publications, August 1999. See also Robert J. Kuglin, *The Toronto Blessing: What Would the Holy Spirit Say?* (Camp Hill, PA: Christian Publications, 1996).

About the Authors

Richard Abanes is the Founder/Director of Religious Information Center, a ministry which provides information on cults, the occult, world religions and various religious movements.

Frank Chan, MA, ABD, is Professor of Bible at Nyack College, Nyack, NY.

Elio Cuccaro, Ph.D., is Professor of Theology and Ministry at Nyack College, Nyack, NY and Senior Editor at Christian Publications, Camp Hill, PA.

Daniel J. Evearitt, Ph.D., is Associate Professor of Religion and Theology at Toccoa Falls College, Toccoa Falls, GA.

K. Neill Foster, Ph.D., is Executive Vice President/Publisher of Christian Publications, Inc., in Camp Hill, PA, the publishing house of The Christian and Missionary Alliance.

Stephen Julian, Ph.D., is Professor of Communications at Nyack College, Nyack, NY.

Harold P. Shelly, Ph.D., is Professor of Church History and Religions at Alliance Theological Seminary, Nyack, NY.

Ronald Walborn, D.Min., is Assistant Professor of Pastoral Ministry at Nyack College, Nyack, NY.